Literature in Perspective

General Editor: Kenneth Grose

Gerard Manley H▢▢▢▢

Literature in Perspective

Gerard Manley Hopkins

Jim Hunter

Evans Brothers Limited London

Published by Evans Brothers Limited
Montague House, Russell Square, London, W.C.1

© Jim Hunter 1966

First published 1966

Third reprint 1975

Set in 11 on 12 pt. Fournier and printed in Great Britain by

Tinling (1973) Ltd, Prescot, Merseyside

(A member of the Oxley Printing Group)

SBN 237 44688 x limp   PRA 4080

SBN 237 44687 1 cased

Literature in Perspective

Reading is a pleasure; reading great literature is a great pleasure, which can be enhanced by increased understanding, both of the actual words on the page and of the background to those words, supplied by a study of the author's life and circumstances. Criticism should try to foster understanding in both aspects.

Unfortunately for the intelligent layman and young reader alike, recent years have seen critics of literature (particularly academic ones) exploring slender ramifications of meaning, exposing successive levels of association and reference, and multiplying the types of ambiguity unto seventy times seven.

But a poet is 'a man speaking to men', and the critic should direct his efforts to explaining not only what the poet says, but also what sort of man the poet is. It is our belief that it is impossible to do the first without doing the second.

LITERATURE IN PERSPECTIVE, therefore, aims at giving a straightforward account of literature and of writers—straightforward both in content and in language. Critical jargon is as far as possible avoided; any terms that must be used are explained simply; and the constant preoccupation of the authors of the Series is to be lucid.

It is our hope that each book will be easily understood, that it will adequately describe its subject without pretentiousness so that the intelligent reader who wants to know about Donne or Keats or Shakespeare will find enough in it to bring him up to date on critical estimates.

Even those who are well read, we believe, can benefit from a lucid expression of what they may have taken for granted, and perhaps—dare it be said?—not fully understood.

K. H. G.

Gerard Manley Hopkins

A year or two ago someone remarked that the poet seen more than any other on the shelves of undergraduates was Gerard Manley Hopkins. The primary reason for this is, one imagines, the challenging originality of style and statement which is clear from any page of Hopkins's work. This poet is very different from others, and when the reader begins to suspect that his poetry is also very good, he wants to meet the challenge and gain a real understanding. This book is intended to enable him to do that, whether or not he is a student of literature and whether or not he reads more profound books on the subject later.

Where poems are identified here by numbers, they refer to the Fourth Edition (edited by W. H. Gardner and N. H. Mackenzie) of the *Poems of Gerard Manley Hopkins*, published in Oxford Paperback. Most readers, however, will meet Hopkins first in a selection, such as the Penguin (also edited by Gardner) or the Heinemann edition edited by James Reeves; and although these are indeed selections from Hopkins's total work, they both include all his finished mature poetry: forty-nine poems from *The Wreck of the Deutschland* to the sonnet *To R.B.*, which are (I believe) always printed in the same order. The present book is not a scholar's commentary, but the superficial difficulty of Hopkins's poetry has made it desirable to give some attention, though brief, to as many individual poems as possible. This is not to say that all difficulties are explained away, but simply that an attempt has been made, for nearly every mature poem, to note its basic outline and clarify the major awkwardnesses.

In the central chapters of the book, then, the poems are examined, in approximately chronological order. These are preceded by a biographical chapter (with a regrettably short account of the Letters) and a chapter relating Hopkins to his times: these should probably be read first. After the chronological survey of the poetry and a brief description of the early poems, notebooks, and fragments, come three general chapters giving the more detailed account necessary of Hopkins's versification, words and word-order, and imagery. A brief last chapter describes some critical attitudes to Hopkins.

The bibliography at the end of the book should be taken also as a list of books from which I may have borrowed insights and observations; these are not normally acknowledged in the text. In the second impression I have made several corrections suggested to me by, amongst others, Dr. Andor Gomme and Mrs. Pamela Hawker, to whom I am very grateful. My greatest debt is to Kenneth Grose, himself a lifelong student and teacher of Hopkins's poetry, to whose editorial kindness I have repeatedly been thankful to turn.

J. H.

Acknowledgements

The portrait of Gerard Manley Hopkins and the facsimile of *Harry Ploughman* are taken from *The Letters of Gerard Manley Hopkins to Robert Bridges*, edited by C. C. Abbott, and the two drawings by the poet are from *The Journals and Papers of Gerard Manley Hopkins*, edited by H. House and G. Storey. The author and publishers are indebted to the Oxford University Press for permission to reproduce these illustrations and the extracts from Hopkins's poems, letters and journals. Extracts from 'The Poetry of Gerard Manley Hopkins' from the volume *The Function of Criticism: Problems and Exercises*, by Yvor Winters are reprinted by permission of the publisher Alan Swallow (British Commonwealth rights excluding Canada: Routledge and Kegan Paul; copyright 1957 Yvor Winters).

Contents

The Author

Jim Hunter, M.A., is Senior English Master at Bristol Grammar School. He is the author of four novels, *The Flame*, *The Sun in the Morning*, *Sally Cray* and *Earth and Stone*, and a previous volume in this seriës, *The Metaphysical Poets*. He has also edited two school anthologies of modern fiction.

I

The Life and Letters

Gerard Manley Hopkins was born in 1844, the eldest child of a London businessman who had just published a book of poems, and of a 'contemplative' mother who was 'a keen student of philosophy, history and politics'. It was a devout Protestant home, one in which the boy would grow up taking for granted the supreme importance in life of religion and the arts. His brothers and sisters confirm this: one sister became an Anglican nun, an uncle was a landscape painter, two brothers won awards for painting and became professional artists, another sister was 'skilled in drawing', and still another sister was, in Hopkins's own words, 'musical beyond the common'. By any standards it was a family of unusual artistic gifts and sensitivity.

With this background Hopkins went to Highgate School, where he received a full nineteenth-century classical education, with its emphasis on religion and literature. He won the poetry prize at school, and was an outstanding scholar. Equally interesting to us is the fragmentary evidence we have of his unusual independence of thought and action, and the strenuous self-discipline which was evident throughout his life. The story of his abstinence for a week from all liquids, simply for a bet, is well-known; and a letter written during his last year at school, to a contemporary who had recently left, gives us a sketch of the school life and gossip which also reveals the writer's character.

This letter (*Further Letters*, pp. 1–5) is headed by a finely-drawn landscape of wild flowers and trees, all within the illuminated 'D' of the conventional 'Dear Luxmoore'. That is 'precious' even by Victorian standards, but the writer was not yet eighteen. The important point to notice is perhaps that although all of us have done equally excessive things at the age of seventeen through enthusiasm, nervousness, or big-headedness, few of us have done them well. (Note also that Hopkins *kept* his no-liquids bet, till he collapsed black-tongued on the playing-field.) The letter-heading is at first disconcerting, then one simply admires. And the letter itself is unpretentious, colloquially at ease, and even, for the age of its writer, mature.

In spite of a nervous humour, which recurs in many of Hopkins's letters and seems often, as it does here, slightly unfortunate, the letter reveals an intense earnestness, both in itself and in the past behaviour it recounts. First Hopkins endeavours 'to dispossess your mind of an extraordinary but deep-seated idea that I wish to give you the cut . . .', so introducing for us the subject of friendship, which was of the keenest importance to Hopkins throughout his life, especially in the isolation which it was necessary for a Jesuit priest to maintain. He is hypersensitive to anything like a 'falling-off' in friendship, or to any imagined charge against him, and always anxious to have it out in the open. This must have been difficult for his friends, and we may feel that it is even foreign to the true nature of friendship, which takes its knocks quietly. Later in this letter Hopkins writes with awful solemnity ('The last blow was this. I extract the account from my journal') of being unjustly treated by a slightly younger boy whom 'it is still my misfortune to be fond of and yet despised by him'; the crisis turns upon whose fault it is that they no longer go for walks together. Hopkins uses words such as 'compromise', 'sacrifice', and 'sowed what I now reaped'. In fairness it should be said that there was probably a suppressed sexual element in the friendship, which would account for the passionate earnestness; but it remains characteristic of an extremism and scrupulosity in Hopkins which we may think were to cause him much unnecessary distress. Father D'Arcy writes (quoted by J. Pick in *Hopkins, Priest and Poet*) of Hopkins's later life, in words which apply also to the poet as a young man:

> In all this he is literal-minded and refuses to distinguish between the serious and the light or fantastic, duty and that happy love which enables the children of God to act in full liberty of spirit.

—and Pick writes of 'a very thin line between Hopkins's conscientious effort to live the Exercises and practise the Rules of the Society [of Jesus] and a certain strain of scrupulosity which had manifested itself even in his Oxford days'.

At times this inability to compromise could appear to the boy's elders as simple stubbornness; and the central section of the letter to Luxmoore is a sensational example. Hopkins relates how he was 'nearly expelled . . . for the most trifling ludicrous little thing which I cannot relate at present'. Dyne (the Headmaster) and he 'had a terrific altercation. I was driven out of patience and cheeked him wildly, and he blazed into me with his riding-whip'. This sounds quite in keeping with the traditions of the English public-school, but it certainly sounds as if it was partly Hopkins's fault also.

Courageous and high-principled the boy seems to have been; he was also not a type that could easily stand being blazed into with a riding-whip. Years later he renewed contact by letter with the Rev. R. W. Dixon, an Anglican priest and poet who had for a short time been a master at Highgate while Hopkins was a pupil there. Dixon's first letter to the Jesuit priest includes this memory of him as a boy:

> I remember a pale young boy, very light and active, with a very meditative and intellectual face, whose name, if I am not vastly mistaken, was yours.

The photograph of Hopkins at nineteen, reproduced on the cover of this book, supports this account: the features are of unusual delicacy, and in many ways resemble those of the stock Victorian image of a poet (after the supposed example of Keats, Shelley and other Romantics); that is, frail, pale and passionate. But note Dixon's word 'active'. Hopkins's character, like his poetry, was of a strength which the 1863 photograph hardly suggests. At no point in Hopkins's life-story do we sense feebleness of character. But his physical frailty was undeniable, and must be borne in mind if we are to understand some of the images and themes in the poetry, as well as the exceptional severity which the Jesuit discipline held for him.

Hopkins entered Balliol College, Oxford, in autumn 1863, and graduated in 1867. These were perhaps the most formative years of his life. He developed his scholarship (achieving a double First in Greek), encountered much of the keenest and most sensitive thought of the time, made a number of close friends including the most important of all, Robert Bridges—and, in 1866, was received into the Roman Catholic Church. The most detailed picture of his Oxford life is the Journal for 1866; there are also various letters, to family and friends, nearly all of some interest, ranging from 'Nurse did not pack my dumb-bells' (his first term at Balliol) to the days of crisis after he had announced his conversion (*Further Letters*).

The portrait which emerges from these writings is profoundly religious, and very literary; but it is characteristic that his Journal should be occupied rather with people and experience (the *stuff* of religion and literature) than with abstract thought. Most of all he records landscape, skies and weather, and does so with the full powers of perceptive imagery which the poet was later to show.

Hopkins's conversion was undoubtedly a decision reached privately. For a long time he had been struggling to defend his remaining in the English Church; theology was to the fore of his mind, and there is every reason to respect the care and steadiness with which he arrived at what remained his confident faith for the rest of his life. In his Journal for 17 July 1866 he writes:

> It was this night I believe but possibly the next that I saw clearly the impossibility of staying in the Church of England, but resolved to say nothing to anyone till three months are over, that is the end of the Long, and then of course to take no step till after my Degree.

In a letter to Urquhart, an Anglican priest leaning towards Rome, he later said: 'when it came [it] was all over in a minute'. The words following are entirely characteristic:

> Again I could not say that your talk influenced me in that direction: to see and hear 'Romanizing' things would throw me back

on the English Church as a rule. In fact . . . for a good time past
I have been uninfluenced by anybody.

One may compare his later remark on studying literary
masterpieces: 'the effect . . . is to make me admire and do otherwise'. With the hindsight which comes from reading his later
works we can see how useless it would have been to argue with
Hopkins about this greatest decision. When he wrote in August
to John Henry Newman, perhaps the most famous and influential
convert to Catholicism in modern English history, it was with
his mind 'made up', but in an anxiety to act with due consideration for his relatives and for his academic obligations. In October
he wrote to his parents with his news. This first letter we do not
have, but the second (16 October), to his father alone, is heavy
with the pain and necessity of hurting his family; this pain leads
to a rigid control of sentence and style which his father's reply
describes as 'harsh and cold'.

He was received into the Catholic Church on 21 October.
There remained one more year of his degree course, at which he
continued steadily, anxious to show his parents and friends that
he was sober of mind and sensible of his responsibilities. In
January 1867 he stayed with Newman at Birmingham, and was
offered a post at the Oratory School there which he took up,
after graduating, in September (but remained only one term).
He was all the time debating whether to become a priest.
Newman urged him to take his time, and it was nearly two years
after his conversion, in May 1868, that he wrote to Newman with
the news that he had decided to enter the Society of Jesus. Again,
the decision was made after full and conscientious debate by a
mind of great intelligence and (for its years) maturity; we must
resist the temptation to say that such a decision was 'wrong' (or
right), and there is no justification for thinking that Hopkins was
not fully aware of the severity of the life he was choosing. To
refuse to respect this decision would be to refuse to respect the
man, and any admiration we showed for his poems would
become condescending and only half-sincere.

The principles of the Society of Jesus are drawn from the Spiritual Exercises of St. Ignatius Loyola, the Spanish founder of the Society, and involve complete self-sacrifice—the giving of the whole life to God, who will know best how to dispose of it. Asceticism (the denial to oneself of all pleasures which are self-centred) had long appealed to Hopkins, and is an important part of the Jesuit discipline. It extends—as is logical but testing—into the intellectual and emotional life. Career as well as comfort is renounced, and such private and personal activity as the writing of poetry is an indulgence which the Jesuit must consider whether he may permit himself. This, at least, was how Hopkins felt about poetry, and in his early ascetic zeal he burned his poems and wrote no more for a period of six or seven years.

The training of a Jesuit is long and arduous, beginning with two years' novitiate dedicated almost entirely to worship, meditation, and the study of only spiritual books. After this period the first vows are taken. Immediately before beginning his novitiate Hopkins holidayed in Switzerland (in July 1868); his Journal for the tour is delightful to read for its word-sketches of landscape and scenery, but silent on religious matters. He then spent several weeks in London with his family, seeing friends and relatives; and on 7 September he entered Manresa House, Roehampton, to begin his training. Of the next two years we necessarily know little; the Journal confines itself mostly to notes on the weather and occasional rich passages of description.

After these two years the novice normally spends several years in wider study, and perhaps teaching; Hopkins went first for philosophical studies to St. Mary's Hall, Stonyhurst, Lancashire, where he remained for three years (1870–1873). Again the Journal is the main guide to his life at this time, though there are a number of letters to his mother, the second of which (2 March 1871), though generally good-humoured and warm, sadly anticipates his later years in Lancashire by such words as: 'everything here is "dank as ditchwater" . . . Except for a cold I am better than usual'. In June 1871 he writes: 'My health is in the main robustious, more so than it has some time been'; but in 1873 he was forbidden to fast during Lent, and 'my work has also been lightened'. This, in a man of twenty-eight, sounds ominous.

For a year, 1873–4, Hopkins returned to Manresa as professor of Rhetoric. Then for three more years, 1874-1877, he studied theology at St. Beuno's College in North Wales. This was probably the happiest period of his life, producing *The Wreck oj the Deutschland* (1876) and the nature sonnets from *God's Grandeur* to *In the Valley of the Elwy* (1877). In 1877 he was ordained priest, at the age of thirty-three.

The Journal stops in 1875, and is for us partly replaced and partly surpassed by the mature poems and letters. The years 1876 and 1877 are a peak in Hopkins's life, representing the full realization of theories he had long pondered, the culmination of his Jesuit training, and the happiest and most sustained poetic inspiration. The Welsh landscape clearly helped:

> The house stands on a steep hillside, it commands the long-drawn valley of the Clwyd to the sea, a vast prospect, and opposite is Snowdon and its range . . . when I see Snowdon and the mountains in its neighbourhood, as I can now, with the clouds lifting, it gives me a rise of the heart.   FURTHER LETTERS pp. 124, 127

For no poet has natural landscape been more important than for Hopkins, and this is perhaps the place to pause in the life-story and attempt an account of his theories on inscape and natural beauty. I put this account in the first chapter because the essence of Hopkins's poetry is missed without an understanding of these theories.

BEAUTY AND INSCAPE

Hopkins's Highgate poems and sketches show a sensitivity to the physical world, and a capacity for distinguishing sensation, which may almost be called abnormal. The literary influence is mainly that of Keats; and although neither Hopkins's poetry nor his prose offer quite the range of mind of the early poet's, in the one matter of accurate and sharply-defined sense-impression he may be thought to outdo Keats. The Oxford poems speak of asceticism, but in a poetry vividly aware of sensation; Hopkins's asceticism is without doubt psychologically linked to his extreme sensitivity. His best-known early poem, *The Habit of Perfection*, is a poem in praise of asceticism; and yet it is a luxurious poem of sensation:

> Nostrils, your careless breath that spend
> Upon the stir and keep of pride,
> What relish shall the censers send
> Along the sanctuary side!
>
> O feel-of-primrose hands, O feet
> That want the yield of plushy sward,
> But you shall walk the golden street
> And you unhouse and house the Lord . . .

It was essential that Hopkins should come to terms with this hypersensitivity to the physical world, for a mind as rigorous as his could not otherwise have supported being enthralled by things mortal. As the poets and religious teachers had endlessly noted, beauty passes; at the end, in Hopkins's own words, 'all is in an unfathomable dark Drowned'.

Hopkins was not likely, in view of his religious leanings, to accept the philosophy of Walter Pater, who was his tutor and with whom he was on good terms at Oxford. Yet it is important for us, as readers of Hopkins, to know about Pater, for in him the undergraduate met one of the more searching minds of the century, and was undoubtedly forced to consider Beauty as a concept fundamental both to art and to life.

Whether knowingly or not, John Keats forty-five years earlier had been responsible for much of this later debate; not only by the texture of his poetry, which is deliberately crowded with sensations, both subtle and unsubtle, but by his exclamation in a letter, 'O, for a Life of Sensations, rather than of Thoughts!', and by the words which close the profound meditation of the *Ode on a Grecian Urn*:

> 'Beauty is Truth, Truth Beauty'—that is all
> Ye know on earth, and all ye need to know.

Pater's interpretation of this tends to be that Beauty is the *only* Truth; his philosophy is (until very late in his life) agnostic, and his conclusion is that since death holds for us no hope, we must seize all of life that we can. 'Not the fruit of experience, but experience itself, is the end.'

Read today, the Conclusion to Pater's book *The Renaissance*, which became a manifesto for the Aesthetic Movement (whose most exotic figure was Oscar Wilde and which some readers will know best through Gilbert and Sullivan's satire on it in *Patience*), seems to betray its inadequacy as a philosophy very obviously. Life is 'this short day of frost and sun'; its brevity is 'awful', and our effort to experience all we can must be 'desperate'. 'We have an interval' before death; 'our one chance lies in expanding that interval, in getting as many pulsations as possible into the given time'. Chance, though, of what? Of 'success in life'. Pater's terms remain vague; he has, indeed, no clear absolutes to which to relate his arguments, and the exhortation is indeed 'desperate', since it exists finally more as a personal statement of the unbearable unsolved problem of mortality than as a coherent philosophy.

For Hopkins that problem did not arise; and at all points he had the sense of eternal absolutes behind the transient reality which delighted him. His Oxford Platonic Dialogue (probably written for Pater), *On the Origin of Beauty*, is of great interest in spite of the aridity intrinsic in such an exercise. After a lengthy exposition of the theory that 'beauty is a relation, and the apprehension of it a comparison' (which in itself implies absolutes), one character (representing one side of the argument) comments that:

> I am either convinced or I really do not know what to say to the contrary; but I am sure there is in the higher forms of beauty—at least I seem to feel—something mystical, something I don't know how to call it.

This contribution is dismissed by the first exponent of the theory, but one senses that Hopkins's sympathies are behind it. It would be natural for him, as a devout Christian, to associate beauty with 'something mystical . . . something beyond'—in short, with an aspect of God. During his Jesuit training his beliefs on this subject clarified themselves, with the aid of his discovery of the medieval theologian Duns Scotus. In the Journal for 19 July 1872 we read:

> At this time I had first begun to get hold of the copy of Scotus on the Sentences [of Lombard] in the Baddely Library and was flush with a new stroke of enthusiasm. It may come to nothing or it may be a mercy from God. But just then when I took in any inscape of the sky or sea I thought of Scotus.

(Note in this passage not only the word 'inscape' but also the close association, in describing revelation or inspiration, of the words 'flush' and 'stroke'. Cf. *Deutschland* 6 and 8.)

Much has been written on Hopkins's use of the word 'inscape'. It occurs frequently in the Journals, often in contexts where no single offered definition will fit. The following notes attempt a brief summary of the theory of *inscape, instress, self* or *sake*, as developed by Hopkins from Duns Scotus.

1. God is 'under the world's splendour and wonder' (*Deutschland* 5); that is, mortal beauty as well as heavenly beauty is a manifestation of God. There are many explicit statements of this, in the 1877 sonnets and in the Journals. The poet's excitement at beauty thus unites with that of the priest, for the significance is the same. And the poet is permitted to love this beauty, provided he recognizes that it is part of the beauty of God. It may even help him to attain the higher beauty. (See the remarks on *The Leaden Echo and the Golden Echo* on pp. 89-90).

2. Everything created has its own distinctive character, which makes it unique and shows God's purpose in creating it. This is its 'self', or 'Thisness' (Scotus's *haecceitas*), marked perhaps by 'sakes' (distinctive features), as in *Deutschland* 22:

> Five! the finding and sake
> And cipher of suffering Christ.

or *Henry Purcell:*

> Let him oh! with his air of angels then lift me, lay me! only I'll
> Have an eye to the sakes of him, quaint moonmarks, to his
>   pelted plumage under
> Wings:

Each thing has, in the words of *The Handsome Heart*, not only its own distinguishing characteristics, but also—

> its own fine function, wild and self-instressed.

'Instressed', we gather (it occurs first in *Deutschland* 5), means 'guided by an instinct or pressure from within'. Instress is the natural urge towards its own proper function, inherent in everything. The instress of the heart is towards God and goodness.

The clearest statement of this doctrine (which is the part particularly derived from Scotus) is in the octet (first eight lines) of the sonnet No. 57 in *Poems:*

> As kingfishers catch fire, dragonflies draw flame;
> As tumbled over rim in roundy wells
> Stones ring; like each tucked string tells, each hung bell's
> Bow swung finds tongue to fling out broad its name;
> Each mortal thing does one thing and the same:
> Deals out that being indoors each one dwells;
> Selves—goes itself; *myself* it speaks and spells;
> Crying *What I do is me: for that I came.*

Notice that, to the sensitive observer, each thing *speaks* of its function, which leads us to—

3. —the revelation of God in the revelation of the 'self' of a thing. This is the ultimate beauty, a moment of oneness or fusion when all the separate qualities of a thing come together to form what it essentially is:

> Brute beauty and valour and act, oh, air, pride, plume, here
> Buckle! AND the fire that breaks from thee then. . . .
>
> THE WINDHOVER

'Thee' here is Christ, who reveals himself in the instant when the poet perceives the separate characteristics of the bird as essentially one. Some words of Pater, from an essay on *The School of Giorgione*, may be worth quoting here:

> All art constantly aspires towards the condition of music. For while in all other works of art it is possible to distinguish the matter from the form, and the understanding can always make this distinction, yet it is the constant effort of art to obliterate it. ... In its ideal, consummate moments, the end is not distinct from the means, the form from the matter, the subject from the expression.

There is much here that is applicable to Hopkins's poetry, which itself 'constantly aspires towards the condition of music'. In the 'ideal, consummate moments' of inscape the various elements of experience come triumphantly together, and God is seen there.

4. The word 'inscape' was coined by Hopkins presumably as a more general version of terms such as 'landscape' and 'seascape', which mean an assembly of different elements (tree, house, fields, hedge, sky, etc.) seen as one. The prefix 'in-' suggests the insight into the essential nature of the subject, or the inner impact it has upon the beholder. *Inscape* then may be used to mean:

(a) that in a thing which reveals God; the thing in its function, when its self or pattern is discernible ('design, pattern, or what I am in the habit of calling "inscape" is what I above all aim at in poetry').

(b) the experience of perceiving this. Hopkins sometimes uses the word as a verb: 'Then I inscaped the whole', i.e. 'I gathered the separate aspects of the thing together and achieved a sense of the whole, of its individuality, its function, the hand of God behind it'. The danger of course is that one can continue one's paraphrase almost indefinitely; and it must be admitted that Hopkins is very free in his use of the word 'inscape' in different contexts (it does not, however, occur in the poetry).

This is the theory which had matured in Hopkins's thought by the time he began writing poetry again. It finds its way into his first and greatest mature poem, *The Wreck of the Deutschland*; one might say 'insists itself', for the stanza concerned (5) is only *just* relevant to the rest of the poem.

> I kiss my hand
> To the stars, lovely-asunder
> Starlight, wafting him out of it; and
> Glow, glory in thunder;
> Kiss my hand to the dappled-with-damson west:
> Since, tho' he is under the world's splendour and wonder,
> His mystery must be instressed, stressed;
> For I greet him the days I meet him, and bless when I under-
> stand.

The story of the writing of this great poem is told by Hopkins in a letter to Canon Dixon, 5 October 1878:

> You ask, do I write verse myself. What I had written I burnt before I became a Jesuit and resolved to write no more, as not belonging to my profession, unless it were by the wish of my superiors; so for seven years I wrote nothing but two or three little presentation pieces which occasion called for. But when in the winter of '75 the Deutschland was wrecked in the mouth of the Thames and five Franciscan nuns, exiles from Germany by the Falck Laws, aboard of her were drowned I was affected by the account and happening to say so to my rector he said that he wished someone would write a poem on the subject. On this hint I set to work, and, though my hand was out at first, produced one.

One has reason to be grateful to the rector at St. Beuno's; and it is quite possible that he knew of Hopkins's inclination towards poetry and was anxious to relieve him of his scruples. Hopkins seized the opportunity, and worked as if it were the last as well as the first poem of his maturity. There is no hint of his hand being out, but rather an extraordinary technical intricacy which must be the fruit of infinite pains; moreover, it appears to be an attempt to say almost everything he wanted at that time to say—

not only, that is, about the nuns, but about his own conversion and difficulties, about inscape (the heart of the poem is the nun's 'reading' of God as engineer of the storm, the recognition that he was behind everything), about God's kindness through cruelty, and about Britain's estrangement from the Catholic faith. There are very few aspects of Hopkins's later poetry which are not anticipated by the *Deutschland*; and although it is natural for us to marvel that so huge a poem should be a poet's first for seven years, it is probable that but for the accumulated inspiration of that time Hopkins would not have achieved something so large or powerful.

Perhaps the rector, though doubtless puzzled by the poem's complexities, congratulated Hopkins on the achievement and urged him to write other poems. At all events, the months before Hopkins's ordination in 1877 produced a series of sonnets with inscape as their theme, which are Hopkins's happiest and most consistent group of poems, though there is perhaps some waning of inspiration as the summer progresses.

PRIESTHOOD

In September 1877 he was ordained, and began four years of shifting priesthood, in various parts of the country. These duties he never found easy, particularly in the large industrial cities of Lancashire, where he was sickened by his sense of 'the hollowness of this century's civilization'. At intervals from 1879 onwards there are outbursts in his letters against either the ugliness of the cities or the weariness of his work.

> I never could write; time and spirits were wanting; one is so fagged, so harried and gallied up and down. And the drunkards go on drinking, the filthy, as the scripture says, are filthy still ...
> To Bridges, 26 October 1880

Yet the accounts of those who knew him, and the evidence of several poems written between 1879 and 1883, show that, whatever his difficulties, he was a comfort and a guide to those he dealt with. The gentle yet brisk tone of *Spring and Fall, Felix Randal, The Handsome Heart* and *The Bugler's First Communion* are consistent with the comment of a Jesuit contempora

> What struck me most of all in him was his child-like guilelessn~~
> and simplicity, his gentleness, tender-heartedness, and his lovi~~
> compassion for the young, the weak, the poor, and for all who
> were in any trouble or distress.

In October 1881 he returned to Manresa for the Tertianship,
'the third year (really ten months) of noviceship which we under-
go before taking our last vows'. This was a second period of
seclusion: 'I see no newspapers, read none but spiritual books';
but it was a relief and refreshment after the hard pastoral work of
1879–1881. After the Tertianship he became a teacher at Stonyhurst; and then, in 1884, was elected Fellow (in Classics) of the
Royal University of Ireland.

Although these posts saved Hopkins from the hardships of all-
weather visiting, often in infected homes and smoky streets
which were dangerous to a man of his frailty, they trapped him
in a heavy routine of academic duties which he found almost
overwhelming, at least in Dublin.

> I have a salary of £400 a year, but when I first contemplated the
> six examinations I have yearly to conduct, five of them running,
> and to the Matriculation there came up last year 750 candidates,
> I thought that Stephen's Green (the biggest square in Europe)
> paved with gold would not pay for it...
>
> To Bridges, 7 March 1884

He remained in this post until his death, of typhoid, in June
1889; and for much of the time was in a state of extreme depression, a condition both mental and physical. The poems of this
time, though few, are perhaps his most famous, and are discussed in Chapter Six. Even in their desolation, and in his letters
of the period, courage and good-humour struggle to keep control; and in the last few months the tone becomes one of great
fortitude, of acceptance, though reluctant, that he is fated to be
'time's eunuch', lonely, unproductive, and without prospect of
making full use, in the world of men, of his gifts. He had long
renounced the possibility of worldly glory, and opposed on

several occasions the efforts of friends to publish his work; yet he also wrote that:

> fame, the being known, though in itself one of the most dangerous things to man, is nevertheless the true and appointed air, element, and setting of genius and its works. What are works of art for? to educate, to be standards . . . it is the true rule for dealing in them, what Christ our Lord said of virtue, Let your light shine before men that they may see your good works and glorify your Father in heaven.
>
> To Bridges, 13 October 1886

And from the last sonnet, *To R.B.*, it is clear that he tended, at the end, to see his life—artistically—as a failure. Had Bridges not kept and (in 1918) published his poetry, it might have been so; for amongst many earnest attempts in other directions, he found he could 'not breed one work that wakes', and the extreme drudgery of academic life, with his failure to find valuable or stimulating friendship, was indeed a waste of his exceptional talents.

The depression, however, is more severe than this alone accounts for. Public taste being what it is, the last poems have become Hopkins's most-admired for the fierce impression they leave on the reader of one man's acute agony and self-hatred. They are poems of sickness, composed by an intelligence keen enough to know that it was itself awry, and to endeavour to fight towards health. It is only natural—indeed essential—that we should seek the causes of this disorder.

In the 1930s there was something approaching a feud between Protestant or agnostic critics, who maintained that Hopkins's desolation at this time was a tragic and direct result of the severe Jesuit discipline, and Jesuit critics, who pointed out that this spiritual 'aridity' is a common experience of 'many who have travelled the road of the spiritual life' (Pick) and see it as sent from heaven. Hopkins himself, at almost all points, defends God's apparent cruelty in imposing suffering:

> Thou art lightning and love, I found it, a winter and warm
> DEUTSCHLAND 9

Why? That my chaff might fly; my grain lie, sheer and clear.

CARRION COMFORT

It seems to me certain that Hopkins himself remained all his life convinced of the rightness of his choice of life, and of the watchful care of God. If this was the way God willed it, this was the way it must be; and, although at moments in the last poems he protests, it is with humility and respect: 'Thou art indeed just, Lord. . .'. He was also well aware that his distress resulted, as mental distress most often does, from aspects of his own character; the most terrible of the last sonnets is perhaps *I wake and feel the fell of dark—*

> God's most deep decree
> Bitter would have me taste; my taste was me;

—where the claustrophobia of knowing and communicating only with oneself gasps out in a climax of self-disgust. And it is the poet's own character that one may usefully look at to understand his last distress. The causes here are clear and uncontroversial.

Firstly, he was always physically frail. Throughout his life there are brief references in his letters to a recent illness, or to exhaustion. Although the letters and Journals do not suggest mental distress in his youth, *The Wreck of the Deutschland* (stanzas 1–3) emphatically does; and the spiritual crisis is expressed in characteristically physical terms:

> Thou hast bound bones and veins in me, fastened me flesh,
> And after it almost unmade, what with dread,
>   Thy doing: . . .

> I did say yes
> O at lightning and lashed rod . . .
> Thou knowest the walls, altar and hour and night:
> The swoon of a heart that the sweep and the hurl of thee trod
>   Hard down with a horror of height:
> And the midriff astrain with leaning of, laced with fire of stress.

This imagery recurs in his work, and when associated with his admiration for physical strength in others—the sailors of the *Deutschland* and the *Eurydice*, Felix Randal, Harry Ploughman —and the values implied in his praise of Dryden's writings ('the naked thew and sinew of the English language') suggest that his frailty was not a difficulty we should underestimate.

Some critics feel that there is a masochistic trend in Hopkins's imagery (see Chapter Ten); and most readers recognize a nervous excitement of one sort or another in Hopkins's interest in shipwreck, battle, and suicide or self-mutilation. One should perhaps quote part of an extraordinary letter to Bridges, of 7 September 1888:

> It seems to me I can not always last like this: in mind or body or both I shall give way—and all I really need is a certain degree of relief or change; but I do not think that what I need I shall get in time to save me. *This reminds me* [my italics] of a shocking thing that has just happened to a young man well known to some of our community. He put his eyes out.

The description proceeds with some precision, and concludes:

> I mention the case because it is extraordinary: suicide is common.

This is immediately followed by another story of a medical student going 'astray'. In the previous month Hopkins had written to Bridges of having enjoyed R. H. Dana's *Two Years Before the Mast*; he complains of technical details of seamanship which he cannot understand:

> there are other things, though, as a flogging, which is terrible and instructive *and it happened*—ah, that is the charm and the main point.

His letters and Journals record the sudden deaths—most of them suicides—of an extraordinary number of his Oxford friends; and this, rather than testifying to Hopkins's morbidity, may serve to remind us that he was not alone in his generation in suffering such depression, and that he withstood it with greater fortitude than some. His letter to Baillie, of 24 April 1885, remarks:

> Three of my intimate friends at Oxford have thus drowned themselves, a good many more of my acquaintances and contemporaries have died by their own hands in other ways: it must be, and the fact brings it home to me, a dreadful feature of our days.

In the same letter he writes:

> The melancholy I have all my life been subject to has become of late years not indeed more intense in its fits but rather more distributed, constant, and crippling . . . It is useless to write more on this: when I am at the worst, though my judgment is never affected, my state is much like madness.

As a creative artist and a man capable (as his letters and poems show) of warm love, Hopkins needed to give and be received, to reach others and enrich his own life in enriching theirs. The excellence and fullness of his correspondence with Robert Bridges and R. W. Dixon is in great part due to its uniqueness. There were no other friends of this kind, no other frequent correspondents at all. Yet Hopkins was strongly drawn towards people. Even his letters from Ireland include appreciative notes of those he has met or been amused by. From Lancashire in 1879 he writes:

> the houses red, mean, and two storied; there are a dozen mills or so, and coalpits also; the air is charged with smoke as well as damp; but the people are hearty.

At Oxford in his youth he wanted to know everyone, and was drawn to complete strangers by their features:

> His face was fascinating me last term: I generally have one fascination or another on. Sometimes I dislike the faces which

fascinate me but sometimes much the reverse, as is the present case.

From remarks like this last and others in the prose it is sometimes suggested that there was a tinge of the homosexual in Hopkins, and that this, being deeply repressed, contributed to the tensions which troubled him psychologically. The question cannot be answered, and is almost irrelevant: whatever of sexual impulse came to Hopkins had (because of the life he had chosen) to be sublimated, and undoubtedly was. The tension would exist in any case. 'A single life', he wrote to Bridges after the latter's becoming engaged, 'is a difficult, not altogether a natural life; to make it easily manageable special provision, such as we have, is needed . . .'

The 'we' here presumably refers to Jesuits. Special provision or not, the lack of anyone with whom Hopkins could *share* his mature years, his difficulties in Liverpool and in Dublin, was plainly a severe hardship.

The solution was to create in words, and to share his life with God. But in Dublin neither of these seemed regularly possible. He could not sustain work begun, could not recapture the driving inspirations of earlier years: the exceptions to this are the few 'terrible' sonnets, which 'came like an inspiration, unbidden and against my will'. During his last years he composed music, began theological and classical theses, worked on his verse-tragedy *St. Winefred's Well*, and began poems; but nothing of any size was completed. And although he could recognize his illness for what it was (as in the letter to Baillie quoted above, which is an admirably clinical account), he was sufficiently prisoner to it to feel that God was cold to him for some reason he could not understand. In the face of such a sensation, his constant efforts to cheer himself and avoid boring or grieving his correspondents are impressive. His last letter, a few weeks before his death, opens:

I am ill today, but no matter for that, as my spirits are good . . .

Hopkins's letters to Bridges and Dixon are among the best in English, in spite of their limited range of subject-matter and feeling. The correspondence with Bridges is lengthy and frequent from 1877 till Hopkins's death in 1889; that with Dixon begins in 1878 and is regular thereafter. Since the *Deutschland* was written in 1875–6, these two volumes of correspondence cover almost the whole of Hopkins's poetic career.

Bridges, who collected Hopkins's poems and published them twenty-nine years after their author's death, was at Oxford with Hopkins, then became a doctor, and was finally Poet Laureate. His poetry, though not much read today, was widely admired in Edwardian times. The *Testament of Beauty*, on which he worked in his old age, was a long philosophical poem, the fruit of much meditation. As a man he was much more worldly and casual than Hopkins, with a good intellect and a sensitive response to literature of the past, but very little understanding of Hopkins's poetry. His own letters to Hopkins, except the very last, do not survive.

Dixon, an altogether less sophisticated man, was a country parson for most of his life, but published several volumes of poetry, and a History of the Church, without winning fame. His great gentleness and humility make his remarks on Hopkins's poetry more appreciative than those of Bridges, and in places they also show some understanding.

To these two men Hopkins wrote of himself and his work, and above all of poetry. He explained his own poems—sometimes the notes he made are still of use to us—and enclosed them in manuscript (otherwise we should not have them at all). He wrote at length on the poetry of Bridges and Dixon, with much praise but also with sharp queries or rebukes, and he wrote about English literature past and present. His letters contain shrewd assessments or appreciations of Tennyson, Keats, Shelley, Wordsworth, Swinburne, Milton, Goethe, Dante, Poe, Hardy, Doughty, Vaughan, Marvell, Herbert, Blake, George Eliot, Dickens, Morris, Surrey, R. L. Stevenson, Thomas Campbell, Barnes of Dorset, Walt Whitman, Burns, Carlyle, Mrs. Gaskell,

Langland, Dryden, Ovid, and 'that scarecrow misbegotten Browning crew' who, he admits, 'are very fine too in their ghastly way'. His remarks seem to us apter than those of almost any other Victorian critic; his strongly independent mind gives his criticism a disinterested and searching force, and (as in the letters of Keats and Lawrence) the informal context allows for a colloquial statement of his exact feelings, which the tone of a more academic or journalistic review would tend to falsify.

The individual judgments are striking and valuable, and, as one would expect, they illumine Hopkins's own poetic practice. His description of Andrew Marvell as 'a most rich and nervous poet'—using the word 'nervous' in praise—is both a superb insight into the metaphysical poet and a clue to Hopkins himself. (It means, I think, 'alive to sensation, to the *nerves*', but the modern connotation is probably there also.) On Swinburne:

> . . . a perpetual functioning of genius without truth, feeling, or any adequate matter to be at function on. There is some heavy-dom, in long waterlogged lines (he has no real understanding of rhythm, and though he sometimes hits brilliantly at other times he misses badly) . . .

Even more interesting are the general judgments on poetry. Many remarks will be quoted in other chapters: the following are worth printing now, to show at once the rigour and integrity of Hopkins's literary thinking:

> A true humanity of spirit, neither mawkish on the one hand nor blustering on the other, is the most precious of all qualities in style. . . . After all, it is the breadth of his human nature that we admire in Shakespeare.
>
> To Dixon, 12 October 1881

> The effect of studying masterpieces is to make me admire and do otherwise. So it must be on every original artist to some degree, on me to a marked degree.
>
> To Bridges, 25 September 1888

A kind of touchstone of the highest or most living art is serious-ness, not gravity but the being in earnest with your subject—reality.

To Bridges, 1 June 1888

there may be genius uninformed by character. I sometimes wonder at this in a man like Tennyson: his gift of utterance is truly golden, but go further home and you come to thoughts commonplace and wanting in nobility. . . . In Burns there is . . . richness and beauty of manly character . . . but a great want in his utterance.

To Bridges, 22 October 1879

Hopkins's letters do not often touch on spiritual matters. Dixon was a Protestant and Bridges not a religious man at all. When he does permit himself such a remark it is characteristically firm. The following passage has a humbling directness:

The poem [Bridges's *O my vague desires*] is autobiographical, as you would say; it tells of what you really feel in yourself. What then is the meaning of those yearnings or aspirations in the mind? You bear witness against yourself that you have them. And, as you suggest in one of your sonnets, if they are powerfully felt even now, when the mind is drawn off them and engrossed by so many things, it is likely they will be at some other time its whole life and being, whether they are gratified or not gratified. . . . You cannot wisely neglect this world of being to which you imply that you will come. In it or above it is the sovereign spirit God, to whom you should now at once make your approach with the humblest and most earnest prayers.

To Bridges, 26 January 1881

Hopkins's letters, taking over as they do from the Journals, are really his best biography. The ill health is hinted at early and reappears more and more persistently. But almost always any complaint is accompanied by a mustering of himself into labori-ous humour or new hope, e.g. in Michaelmas 1887:

The eyes are almost out of my head. Also I am at [composing] a fugue, of which I have great hopes. . . .

or this, from the middle of a letter of September 1888:

Can there be gout or rheumatism of the eyes? If there can I have it. I am a gouty piece now.
Gouty rhymes to Doughty.

(and he proceeds to discuss that poet).

Hopkins's sense of humour should be noted, especially in view of his repudiation (see above) of 'gravity'; compare his description of Newman, in the letter of 24 September 1866, as—

most kind, I mean in the very best sense, for his manner is not that of solicitous kindness but genial and almost, so to speak, unserious.

Hopkins liked riddles, puns, and anecdotes (most of which seem unfunny to modern readers) partly because this was a taste of the time, and more, perhaps, because of his interest in anything odd—'all things counter, original, spare, strange'. This is linked to the persistent word-play in his poetry. In his letters the humour is most frequently there out of consideration for his reader, a wish to be agreeable rather than over-solemn or depressed.

The whole picture is of strength, sensitivity, and generosity; the weakness is the sad one he could not help, a certain narrowness of scope and subject. Hopkinsian oddity is there, but is always subordinated to intellectual integrity and to humanity. There are many places, in the life-story, the letters, and the poetry, where Hopkins comes near to failure in the wilds of eccentricity, distress, or cleverness; but always a largeness of heart, a looking-outward to others, and an intense humility before God, vindicates him and turns the risk into an unusual excellence. As he himself wondered whether genius could exist without a noble character, so he himself emerges as a great man, and therefore the greater poet.

2

Hopkins within his Age

Hopkins's poems were first published in 1918, and had some influence on English and American poetry in the next twenty or thirty years. Even today, a reader opening a book of Hopkins for the first time may think (a) this is very odd stuff, and (b) this is very 'modern'. For a long time people's notions of Hopkins's dates seemed hazy, for this reason. This chapter is designed to set Hopkins in his time (the middle of Victoria's reign), not so much for the sake of historical accuracy as because this makes the approach to his work easier. He was a Victorian, writing in the spirit and with the interests of his own age, and until this is realized, one's picture of the poet will not be true.

Between us and the eighteenth century is a century and a half of very rapid change in human society. Although there is scarcely a decade in the period without its own innovation or discovery, the vast differences between our own age and the eighteenth century may be attributed to two developments above all: the Industrial Revolution, and the Romantic Movement. In the latter should be included the new political pressures of republicanism and socialism.

These two major changes caused much upheaval in the early decades of the nineteenth century. By Hopkins's time they were to a large extent accepted. Ugly industrial cities with large homogeneous populations were seen as part of 'normal' life; in the arts the reaction against eighteenth-century decorum and rationalism was complete; and although socialism was still suppressed, there was beginning a general recognition that the poor and uneducated masses deserved better treatment. The popularity of Dickens's novels indicates an audience which, if not truly dissatisfied with capitalism, permitted itself at least the luxury of sympathy with the downtrodden. The attitudes of the thinking man (to industry, or the arts, or politics) in Hopkins's day were already closer to our own than to those of the preceding century; but in Hopkins's day they were still new.

THE INDUSTRIAL REVOLUTION

Of this little need be said; its impact was clear enough, and Hopkins's own letters, together with the poems *God's Grandeur*, *The Sea and the Skylark*, and *Tom's Garland*, offer protests perhaps more heartfelt and certainly more spontaneous than those of Dickens (though the latter's *Hard Times* is of interest to us as a compelling account of a Lancashire town of exactly the kind Hopkins worked in at intervals from 1877 till 1881). A Victorian poet, with his eyes newly opened by his Romantic predecessors to the impulses from a vernal wood or the meanest flower that blows, found himself writing just at the time when whole landscapes were disappearing under brick and pavement, erupting into slag heaps, or retreating before the railway. The effect of this was to augment still further the Victorian's reverence for natural landscape, which degenerated eventually into the Green-Belt poetry which until recently overpowered school anthologies and is still current in women's magazines.

Hopkins, the best Victorian nature-poet, involves himself most intensely in the life of natural things, but almost always avoids falseness of sentiment. There is a sincerity in his reverence for the sea and the skylark, and in his horror at the 'sordid turbid time', which most poets who make such protestations tend to lack. Theirs are poems by suburb-dwellers for city-dwellers: nature is visited and admired and kept in her place. Hopkins sees town-life as the excrescence, the unreality.

ROMANTICISM

To Romanticism some sort of general reference must be made. Readers with a thorough knowledge of what Romanticism was are invited to skip the next page or so. The Romantic movement was perhaps the most important single revolution in Western culture, rivalled only by the Renaissance. Victorian literature, like the music and art of the time, is essentially and almost exclusively Romantic (though the misleading term 'post-Romantic' is sometimes used, to distinguish Victorians from the first Romantics writing at the turn of the century); and Hopkins must be seen as a Romantic poet.

Like most revolutions, Romanticism was both a violent reaction against certain extreme habits of thought of preceding generations, and a full expression of opposite ways of thinking which had been gradually developing at the same time. Thus, though it is clear enough in the Preface to *Lyrical Ballads* (1801) that Wordsworth felt himself to be a revolutionary, in explicit opposition to eighteenth-century poetic diction, as an example of which he instanced Thomas Gray, yet Gray himself in his *Elegy in a Country Churchyard* anticipates other aspects of Romantic thought; and one hundred and fifty years earlier the poetry of Henry Vaughan already showed qualities which, to us, suggest Romantic poetry. In a simplified account, however, we may say that Romanticism was a revolt against eighteenth-century thought, as the following crude tabulation will illustrate.

1. The eighteenth-century thinker placed reason highest among qualities of character and art. The Romantic dedicated himself rather to emotion, spirit and soul.

2. The eighteenth-century took God's existence for granted, and was remarkable for orthodox reverence rather than revelation. Romantic thinkers were sometimes atheists, sometimes Christians, sometimes Pantheists (that is, they believed that everything and everywhere is God; a belief naturally frequent in nature-poetry), but they almost always took religion very seriously, and expected from it some passionate and/or mystical experience.

3. God and man, in the eighteenth-century, gave their highest attentions to mankind, and civilization. The rough places were to be made plain. Trees, flowers and rocks were to be encountered in gardens, not in the open country. The Romantics found God (or 'good') in nature untouched by man: in wild

places, wild creatures, and what they held to be the innocence of childhood.

4. Hence, aristocratic civilization and culture, which were eighteenth-century ideals, seemed of dubious value to the Romantic thinker, who leant rather towards a democratic brotherhood of mankind (cf. the last movement of Beethoven's Ninth Symphony for a widely-known example). The common man—having something of the innocence of the child—showed nobility.

5. In the arts, this meant that decorum, so essential to a good eighteenth-century creation, might be deliberately abandoned, in the interests of a wider range of expression and experience, and—in diction—of a deeper sincerity. All manner of sensation was to be explored, by the Romantic, and savoured (this idea is pressed to its drastic conclusions later in the century).

6. Whereas eighteenth-century thought interested itself most in society, the Romantic set supreme importance upon individual experience. The typical Romantic experience was solitary; in such a state the life of the emotions (or sensations) could be most intensely appreciated, and—more profoundly—contact with God, or Truth, or Nature, might be achieved. Direct contact became the aim, rather than shared social enjoyment; this was reflected in a change of attitude towards the reading of poetry, which became a private and dangerously religiose occupation in some circles.

Each of these principles is vital to Hopkins's personality and work. It is not (1) as a sage that he wins our admiration, but as a man of rare force and delicacy of passion. His religion (2) is inseparable from his whole being, and it deals in sudden revelations, the 'flash from the flame to the flame', the beacon shining 'across my foundering deck' in the midst of storm. God is revealed to Hopkins (3) in the natural personality (inscape) of things: several times the poet deplores cities, and the words 'brute' and 'wild' are for Hopkins words he uses with delight.

Repeatedly he returns to the theme of childhood (4), of 'innocent mind and Mayday in girl and boy'; and the only adults he writes of are simple 'Jacks', working-men such as Felix Randal or the sailors, whose natural decency is not complicated by education. No reader of Hopkins will fail to notice (5) his departures from traditional decorum, his extraordinary reshuffling of the resources of English; and (6) few writers have lived—particularly as regards literary communication—in more complete isolation than Hopkins. In one of his records of a walk made in company he says that he has to be alone in order to appreciate a landscape, and when we are moved to pity his loneliness we must realize that it was to a great extent voluntary, and that it made possible his most exalting experiences, as well as his most tragic.

THE LITERARY BACKGROUND

Hopkins is closer, in terms of intention and even method, to the early Romantics than to any one poet of his own day. This is perhaps mainly a matter of stature. Amongst Hopkins's contemporaries the popular poets, such as Tennyson and Browning, hardly ever show what Hopkins called 'the being in earnest with your subject: reality', or what another contemporary, Matthew Arnold, called 'high seriousness'; while those, like Arnold, of more sober intention, lacked not only the powerful inspiration of Hopkins but also the virtuosity of Tennyson or Browning.

The reader of Hopkins ought to know something, first, of the poetry and ideals of Keats, Shelley, and Wordsworth; the following notes are an attempt to help, but they will inevitably mean more to the experienced reader of Romantic poetry.

Shelley's is the least potent influence. Hopkins's philosophy was in no sense revolutionary, and the Prometheus-Shelley, liberating mankind from ancient tyrannies, quickening a new birth over the universe, would not have direct relevance for him. But Shelley's popularity in the nineteenth century depended rather upon the special energy of his lyricism, the exciting sweep of rhythm and image which expressed itself in poems about sky, wind, cloud, and light. The self-ordained Victorian successor to

Shelley was Algernon Charles Swinburne, a poet whose alliterative incantations held huge popularity till the First World War, though discriminating readers (such as Hopkins) dissociated themselves at the start from the craze. But in the Hopkins of the *Deutschland*, *The Windhover*, or *Hurrahing in Harvest* there is an unforced surge of energy which is perhaps more truly reminiscent of Shelley. Hopkins's birds, thrusting off earth with a beat of splendid wings, clearly represent Romantic ecstasy or Romantic revelation very much as do Shelley's skylark, or his 'wild' West Wind (the adjective was a favourite of Hopkins also).

This seems far removed from William Wordsworth, who never sought to write Shelley's sort of poetry and might have thought it (and also that of Hopkins) vulgar or immature in its emotional excitability. Wordsworth is a true Romantic, but his upbringing was eighteenth-century, and whatever his experiments in diction and subject-matter (attempting to write about, and in the language of, ordinary men), his poetry possesses always the deeper decorum of considered meditation, composed and balanced statement. For the writing of poetry it was necessary, in Wordsworth's view, that emotion should be 'recollected in tranquillity'; and the spiritual dramas Wordsworth treats are described and pondered with hindsight, not deliberately re-lived. The sudden cry, of ecstasy or pain, which rings out at intervals in Hopkins's poetry, is unimaginable in Wordsworth, in whose work there is a sobriety—perhaps resignation—which Hopkins does not show.

Hopkins was not a great enthusiast of Wordsworth's poetry; their manners are too different. He never quite saw the point of Wordsworth's plainness. Yet their theories of diction agree. Wordsworth's is well-known: the poet is a man like other men, only (as it were) more so; and the language of poetry should be the language actually used by men, though selected and arranged with special skill. Hopkins's dictum is very similar: 'It seems to me that the poetical language of an age should be the current language heightened.' From this agreement the two poets take different ways; but the connection is there. Both refuse to accept the idea that there might be one language for poetry and another for prose; and both turn repeatedly to 'the common man' for inspiration and guidance.

The closer link between the two poets (it is not necessarily an *influence*) is in their abstract thinking. A teacher of many years' experience once remarked to me that he thought Wordsworth was all the time trying to be Hopkins; in other words, that the later poet expressed more strongly and clearly certain intellectual positions which the earlier poet also held. This seems to me a valuable insight into Wordsworth's poetry, especially where he writes of landscape as a moral inspiration; the sonnet *Upon Westminster Bridge* or the ascent of Snowdon in *The Prelude* are, one might say, pure inscape. Hopkins was sensible of the quality:

> What I suppose grows on people is that Wordsworth's particular grace, his *charisma,* as theologists say, has been granted in equal measure to so very few men since time was—to Plato and who else? I mean his spiritual insight into nature. . . .
>
> To Dixon, 7 August 1886

The same phrase 'insight into nature' is applied to Wordsworth in a letter to Dixon five years earlier. Hopkins's most eager praise of Wordsworth, however, is reserved for the great *Ode on Intimations of Immortality from Recollections of Early Childhood.* There are a few men in history, Hopkins says, through whom 'human nature saw something, got a shock.' Like a modern chronicler of the Romantic movement, he recognizes that—

> in Wordsworth when he wrote that ode human nature got another of those shocks, and the tremble from it is still spreading. This opinion I do strongly share; I am, ever since I knew the ode, in that tremble.
>
> To Dixon, 23 October 1886

The ideas of the ode can be seen throughout Hopkins's poetry; 'trailing clouds of glory do we come, from God who is our home' links exactly with Hopkins's sonnet *Spring*, and more generally with many other poems. But it is not simply the ideas of the poem that delight Hopkins so much (the letter to Dixon is a most ardent defence of it against Dixon's attacks, ending 'May the Muses bring you to a better mind'.); 'the execution is so fine' also. The nature of the poem as a great Romantic ode—something which would send a tremble through the nineteenth century—this itself found a response in Hopkins's heart.

Hopkins's link with Keats is of another kind again, and this time one may fairly speak of the later poet's *debt* to the earlier. The *intellectual* stimulus for Hopkins of Keats's poetry would perhaps not be powerful, though the close of the *Ode on a Grecian Urn* ('Beauty is Truth, Truth Beauty') has already been mentioned (p. 18) as an important text for Victorian aestheticians. But Hopkins responded keenly to the remarkable richness of *sense-impressions* crowding the lines of Keats's mature poems. All Victorian poets who are still read today show an awareness of Keats in this respect, even the chaste and Wordsworthian Arnold; a device which suggests the influence is the compound adjective newly coined ('moon-blanch'd night' in Arnold, 'dew-pearl'd' in Browning). But two poets in particular assimilate the example of Keats fully into their own manner and make their own developments from it. One of these is Hopkins; the other is Tennyson, on whom it will be necessary to say more in a moment.

There are plenty of possible examples of Keats's sensuous virtuosity. A reader who has never encountered it might as well plunge straight into the almost licentious indulgence of *The Eve of St. Agnes*, a poem of no intellectual pretensions but a breathless succession of sensations: colour, moonlight, frost, the noise of a feast, the noise of silence, the rustling of silks, the thumping of an amorous heart, the 'snarling' of trumpets, the wind blowing under the carpets in cold stone passages—all linked to a cunningly contrived emotional excitement. Sheer sensation is the end in view, but the whole of Keats's art cannot be dismissed for this reason. In his greater works, as in the poetry of Hopkins, the brilliant rendering of sense-impressions is an attempt to grasp and reach a philosophic understanding of the transience of the physical world.

Hopkins's schoolboy prize poem, *A Vision of the Mermaids*, is openly imitative of Keats, in particular perhaps the narrative poem *Lamia*. Yet already the poet's individuality is evident.

> Plum-purple was the west; but spikes of light
> Spear'd open lustrous gashes, crimson-white; . . .
>
> Anon, across their swimming splendour strook,
> An intense line of throbbing blood-light shook
> A quivering pennon; then, for eyes too keen,
> Ebb'd back beneath its snowy lids, unseen.
>   Now all things rosy turn'd: the west had grown
> To an orb'd rose, which, by hot pantings blown
> Apart, betwixt ten thousand petall'd lips
> By interchange gasp'd splendour and eclipse. . . .

It is superbly done, under the circumstances. It is also already a Hopkins version of Keats: there is a nervous streak in Hopkins which leads him towards surgical imagery ('spikes of light Spear'd open lustrous gashes') and towards an uncomfortably tense drawing-out of sensation. Hopkins's recording of sense-impressions, in all his work, is in fact rarer and more precise than that of Keats; at many points he goes far, perhaps too far, beyond the earlier poet, in imagery of disconcerting extremity, where the reader cannot be expected to master the poet's intention immediately. But Keats's original guidance is still evident. Hopkins's 'lush-kept plush-capped sloe' (*Deutschland* 8), for example, would have struck Keats, as it still strikes many readers, as excessive, frivolous, even 'gimmicky'. Yet the luxurious comparison ('lush' and 'plush') is exactly Keatsian—there is more of Hollywood in Keats than in Hopkins—and so are the compound-adjectives themselves; and as for the assonance, although it is in Hopkins unusually forceful, yet Keats himself is repeatedly conscious of the *sound* of his words:

> with beaded bubbles winking at the brim . . .
>
> . . . and mid-May's eldest child,
> The coming musk-rose, full of dewy wine,
> The murmurous haunt of flies on summer eves.
>
> ODE TO A NIGHTINGALE

(The second example is pirated more than once by Tennyson).

This aspect of Hopkins's verse may be summed up by saying that the 'Hopkins style' (as the new reader will immediately recognize it) owes itself very largely to the poet's appreciation of:

(a) medieval or dialect poems in alliteration and assonance (see Chapter Nine), and

(b) Keats, and those Victorians (Tennyson pre-eminently) influenced by Keats.

Hopkins's attitude to Tennyson himself is complex.

> You call Tennyson 'a great outsider'; you mean, I think, to the soul of poetry. I feel what you mean, though it grieves me to hear him depreciated, as of late years has often been done. Come what may he will be one of our greatest poets . . . When the inspiration is genuine, arising from personal feeling, as in *In Memoriam*, a divine work, he is at his best . . . But . . . he should have called [his *Idylls*] *Charades from the Middle Ages* (dedicated by permission to H.R.H. etc.) . . . His opinions too are not original, often not independent even, and they sink into vulgarity. . . .
>
> To Dixon, 27 February 1879

> his gift of utterance is truly golden, but go further home and you come to thoughts commonplace and wanting in nobility . . .
>
> To Bridges, 22 October 1879

One Keatsian, and popular, aspect of Tennyson is the languid. The last stanza of Keats's *Ode to Autumn* has a dying fall, and a trace—no more—of melancholy (it also has considerable life left in it, but this tended to be missed). *La Belle Dame Sans Merci* and the *Ode to Melancholy* develop the tendency more fully. This is what exerted most influence on Tennyson. Even the Arthurian poems are known best (and deservedly) by *Morte d'Arthur*, with its beautiful evocations of a sad, romantic peace in death, and such poems as *The Lotos Eaters*, *Tithonus*, *Tears, idle tears. . .* , *Ulysses*, or *Break, break, break* . . . take up very fully the mood. An indulgence in languor and melancholy is a characteristic of much Victorian poetry. All too easily for Victorian readers this poetry became a sentimental relief from their prosaic troubles, and the comparatively restrained poem of grief, hinting at courageous suppression of self-pity, at extra-ordinary sensitivities unexpressed, is a commonplace of the time. Hopkins's 'terrible' sonnets are clearly more full-blooded, if nothing else, than those of any contemporary.

Tennyson's skill is in the expression of these hints of infinite passion in poetry of considerable mellifluousness and poise. His verse-lines are smooth and dignified, technically expert, and so is his control of vowels.

> The long day wanes; the slow moon climbs; the deep
> Moans round with many voices.   ULYSSES

> . . . and may there be no moaning of the bar
>   When I put out to sea,

> But such a tide as moving seems asleep,
>   Too full for sound or foam,
> When that which drew from out the boundless deep
>   Turns again home.   CROSSING THE BAR

This skill Hopkins admired; the music of Tennyson's poetry, though subdued, is often admirable, and this interest in sound—in subdued assonances, in alliteration and internal echo—seems widespread in Victorian poetry. Look at the famous lines from *Morte d'Arthur* describing Bedivere's onomatopoeic journey over 'the bare black cliff' and then—

>   on a sudden, lo! the level lake,
> And the long glories of the winter moon.

This is not, of course, really very like Hopkins; but the same devices are being used by Tennyson, in his personal manner. The cruder spirit of Browning has recourse to the same methods:

> And another would mount and march, like the excellent minion
>   he was,
> Aye, another and yet another, one crowd but with many a
>   crest . . .

>   ABT VOGLER

45

With Swinburne alliteration and assonance develop an automatic quality:

> For winter's rains and ruins are over,
> And all the season of snows and sins . . .
>
> Chorus from ATALANTA

Even more important in Swinburne's poetry, however, is the swinging *rhythm*, which was to set Cambridge undergraduates linking arms to chant his works on King's Parade. And this too is a tendency of the time, which finds in Hopkins not a contrary spirit, but its most imaginative and able exponent. We may consider Hopkins's verse-experiments more interesting than those of his contemporaries, but we should note how many of them were experimenting themselves.

Arnold's *Dover Beach* is perhaps the first true free-verse poem by an Englishman. See also Tennyson's hypnotic *Lotos Eaters* or staccato *Light Brigade*, Swinburne's pattering and repetitive stanzas of 'light' lines (that is, light syllables predominate over stressed), Whitman's near-prose incantations, the song-poems of Christina Rossetti and Robert Browning, and Browning's many other experiments, of which the oddest is perhaps the shuffling metre of *A Grammarian's Funeral*:

> Well, here's the platform, here's the proper place.
>   Hail to your purlieus
> All ye high-flyers of the feathered race,
>   Swallows and curlews!

In English poetry one does not encounter metres other than the simple iambic/trochaic (see p. 115 for an explanation of these terms) between the late sixteenth century and the late eighteenth. The Romantic freedom and variety of metre may be to some extent associated with Romantic liking for things medieval. Certainly Hopkins was keenly aware of the metrical liveliness of medieval poetry, and influenced by it; his times in general show a similar tendency, though less bold.

The above literary cross-references have been made to show the place of Hopkins within the literature of his time. Some similar observations may be made about non-literary currents of feeling in the Victorian age.

1. The religious fervour of Romanticism—though it may not always express itself in orthodox Christianity—permeates Victoria's times. Hopkins's conversion to Catholicism was but one of a very large number, especially in the second half of the century, and in some cases (though not that of Hopkins) this rather paradoxically testifies to the currents of doubt that troubled the age. (The convert to Catholicism, it is suggested, is seeking stability, a full code of answers to his perplexities.) Middle-class families grasped religion for the confirmation of their social and moral stability, and the image of the Victorian family governed by a solemn *paterfamilias* who, whatever his private diversions, demanded the highest purity and piety from his wife and children—the image of formal Grace over meals, of morning and evening prayers at which this piety was demonstrated to the servants—is perhaps what comes first to our minds when we hear the word 'Victorian' today. Hopkins's family was such a one, and the father's letter of grief and desperation to Canon Liddon (whose disciple at Oxford Hopkins had been before his doubts of the English Church grew too strong) at the time of his son's conversion shows that here, at least, the religious sincerity was intense. Hopkins lived his whole life among people by whom the supreme importance of religion was taken for granted.

2. As a corollary to this, the psychological tensions which such an upbringing, coupled in many cases with religious and philosophical debate at school and university, could generate in a young man were sometimes severe. In Hopkins's case the difficulty was the reconciling of his conversion with his reluctance to break from his parents and friends. His character was strong enough to enable him to handle the problem with admirable care and firmness. But others were not so strong; and

this same difficulty, or the even harder and more frequent one, that of the young man not fundamentally suited to a pious or even chaste life, who nevertheless endeavoured to grasp God through an overwhelming sense of guilt and frustration, could be disastrous. We have already seen (p. 29) Hopkins's comment on suicide as a feature of his generation. In his somewhat obsessive noting of suicides and madness there seems to be some awareness that he might himself share such tensions. When we read his last poems and letters we understand that (at least ultimately) he did, and only a most powerful self-discipline—to say, as he does often in various ways, 'that way madness lies; let me shun that'—together with a deep trust in God, kept him from similar defeat.

3. Patriotism, associated with this religious conformity, is the other enthusiasm for which the Victorian age is notorious. Britain was, at least in her own eyes, 'top nation': the foreign wars which occurred in Victoria's reign were few enough, far enough away, and successful enough to provide the public with a flattering image of the British soldier and of warfare in general. British colonial expansion did some harm but also some good in what would today be called 'underdeveloped' countries, and from this in turn British trade prospered. The long reign of the Queen, who, because she was a woman, enlisted perhaps more sympathy and therefore more loyalty from her people, and a diplomatic policy of 'splendid isolation', may also account for the particular national pride of the period. Whatever the reasons, the characteristic is undeniable, and vividly apparent to the reader of poetry, if he compares the internationalism or political indifference of the early Romantics with the fervent patriotism of Tennyson, Browning, and Hopkins. In none of these last is the emotion unpleasantly aggressive or self-righteous (as might be said of rather later patriots such as Sir Henry Newbolt); it is more attractive and innocent than that. The excellence of England is taken for granted, and a passionate gratitude is expressed.

> Here and here did England help me; how can I help England? say ...
>
> Browning HOME THOUGHTS, FROM THE SEA

> Our King back, oh, upon English souls!
> Let him easter in us, be a dayspring to the dimness of us, be a
> crimson-cresseted east,
> More brightening her, rare-dear Britain, as his reign rolls . . .
>   Hopkins DEUTSCHLAND

It is an emotion of some importance in Hopkins. His enthusiasm for patriotic songs (of which he composed himself a sufficiently crude example) and 'regimental red'—his assertion in *The Soldier* that if Christ were to be a man on earth again, this would be his trade—will perhaps always surprise us; but his devotion to his native land, intensified by estrangement (first, in the gulf between the national Protestantism and his own Catholicism, and later, by his isolation in Ireland), we can fully understand and respect. It is an element in the significance of *The Wreck of the Deutschland* ('Dame, at our door Drowned'), and a major cause of the poet's distress in the last sonnets. ('England, whose honour O all my heart woos . . .').

Interested readers will observe further kinships between Hopkins and his contemporaries. With most poets it is not necessary to insist in this way on something which is, after all, to be expected. But the originality of Hopkins is so powerful and so attractive that it tends to blind a reader to all else; and when that happens, he is not only more difficult to approach for the first time, but also easy, when better known, to misinterpret.

3

'The Wreck of the Deutschland'

The first poem of Hopkins's maturity is also his greatest, and although all his work is distinctive and unusual, this poem stands quite on its own in literature. There is nothing it closely resembles.

It is a narrative poem, and a dramatic one, which yet contains much theological argument. It is a lengthy poem, but maintains a tempo and tone characteristic of short, urgent lyrics. Though it comes at the start of a poetic career, after a long silence, and though its form is highly original, it yet shows immense assurance and certainty of purpose. The richness and brilliance of the writing in fact give the impression of a skill long practised, reaching a culminating achievement. It is an extreme case of poetic inspiration, in its fullest power and clarity.

In December 1875, the 'Deutschland' ran aground on the Kentish Knock sandbank in the mouth of the Thames. She was bound for America from Germany, carrying emigrants, many of whom were probably refugees from religious persecution. Among them were the five Franciscan nuns whose death is the special point of interest for Hopkins—though, as we shall see, he was concerned for all who died on the ship. Hopkins read newspaper reports of the disaster and discussed it with his superiors at St. Beuno's, where he was studying theology. The poem which resulted is in part a public poem on a recent occurrence, in part a private meditation of great import to the poet. Probably he would not, at that stage, have permitted himself a wholly private poem; at any rate, this is his one poem where he convincingly related his own situation to that of all mankind.

The basic idea of the poem is this: the drowning of the nuns may appear tragic, but in the light of their faith and that of the poet it is certain that God planned it all, and was calling them, by a noble death which, like Christ's, involved drawn-out suffering, to glory in heaven. Furthermore, there is a good chance (Hopkins will not commit himself further than an eager hope) that the example of the nuns, and the exhortations of their leader, may actually have converted to Catholicism and consequent salvation those on board who were not previously practising Catholics. If so, the wreck was a great harvest, showing God's great mercy as well as his omnipotence.

Linked with this argument is a personal statement by the poet, acting as a prologue to the main poem, of his own spiritual struggles before he submitted to God's authority. God gave him a hard time of it, until he submitted, and then the mercy and kindness of God were seen to be unlimited. Part One, which is of ten stanzas, represents this personal account; Part Two (twenty-five stanzas) is the main poem and conclusion.

FORM

This is Hopkins's first substantial poem in what he called 'sprung rhythm'. A full discussion of this rhythm must be left until Chapter Eight: all we need note here is that the poet does not count syllables, but does count stresses. The number of stresses in each line is constant; the number of syllables varies greatly. This allows the poet to make lines slow and heavy (by keeping the number of light syllables in the line to a minimum) or rapid (by placing many light syllables among the stresses). Sprung rhythm is not an obstacle for the reader, unless there is difficulty in seeing *where* the stresses are supposed to be; there are very few places like this in the *Deutschland*. In general a 'straightforward' reading of the poem aloud will at once find out the rhythms intended by the poet. The reader approaching this poem for the first time can reserve his concentration and ingenuity for elucidating the *meaning* of the lines, which is less easily grasped.

The poem is written in eight-line stanzas, rhyming *ababcbca* (a fairly testing rhyme-scheme). The pattern of stresses is:

Line one: 3 stresses (2 in Part One of the poem)
Line two: 3 stresses
Line three: 4 stresses
Line four: 3 stresses
Line five: 5 stresses
Line six: 5 stresses
Line seven: 4 stresses
Line eight: 6 stresses

Stanza 29 therefore scans as follows:

      /   /   /
Ah! there was a heart right
         /   /
There was single eye!
/   /   /   /
Read the unshapeable shock night
      /   /   /
And knew the who and the why;
/   /   /   /   /
Wording it how but by him that, present and past,
/   /   /   /   /
Heaven and earth are word of, worded by?—
    /   /   /   /
The Simon Peter of a soul! to the blast
   / / /   /   /   /
Tarpeian-fast, but a blown beacon of light.

In this form the first four lines make a quatrain which is fairly traditional in shape and can be easily grasped. Frequently this quatrain is separated by punctuation from the rest of the stanza, and this offers an opportunity for epigram, to be more fully glossed in the later lines.

Sister, a sister calling
A master, her master and mine!   19

Five! the finding and sake
And cipher of suffering Christ.

> Mark, the mark is of man's make
> And the word of it Sacrificed.

22

The rest of the stanza consists of longer lines, leading up to the six-stress line at the end; and here Hopkins often works up emotion from the comparative calm of the first four lines to the controlled frenzy which is the most striking characteristic of the poem's tone. The last four lines are frequently an ornate expansion of the first four. The final line, thanks to the freedom afforded by the theory of sprung rhythm, may be slow and weighty, as in stanza 11—

> The sour scythe cringe, and the blear share come.

—or swiftly running as in stanza 25—

> The keener to come at the comfort for feeling the combating keen.

Both, of course, have six and only six stresses. This last line of the stanza, being the longest, lends itself to the fullest possible statement of what has been more tersely expressed earlier (Hopkins is *never* afraid to repeat himself), and so to a feeling of satisfying completeness. Hopkins was perhaps influenced by the stanza used by Spenser in *The Faerie Queen* and copied by Keats and Byron, where the last line is an Alexandrine (twelve syllables) after the pentameters (ten syllables) of those preceding. There are only two cases of running-on from one stanza to another; in the first it is a technical device carefully prepared for ts symbolic effect—

> Thence the discharge of it, there its swelling to be,
> Though felt before, though in high flood yet,
> What none would have known of it, only the heart, being hard at bay,

> Is out with it!   7-8

—and in the second, where the poet is seeking continuity rather than an explosive overflow, the enjambement (running-on) is assisted and smoothed by the carrying-over of rhyme also—

> . . . past all
> Grasp God, throned behind
> Death with a sovereignty that heeds but hides, bodes but abides;
>
> With a mercy that outrides
> The all of water . . .   32–3

The technical attention which has clearly been given to these two enjambements shows how the poet conceived the stanza to be normally a complete and separate whole.

It is hardly necessary to point out the additional brilliances of alliteration, assonance and internal rhyme which mark every line of this poem. Hopkins had been studying Welsh poetry, in which these devices form a system, with rules, known as *cynghanedd*; he is the first poet to use them so extensively in English, but none the less successful for that. Scarcely ever is the sense forced for the sake of the word-pattern, and many times the relationship between key-words is made clear by the bonds of sound, or the balance of paradox accentuated by the poise of the line. Great attention should be paid to the sound of Hopkins's poetry, and reading *The Wreck of the Deutschland* aloud should be a most exciting experience.

This is not an easy poem to elucidate; on the other hand, it is not, as is sometimes feared, absurdly difficult. At every point it will yield up its secrets to the careful reader, and the effort is well worth while. In the following pages I offer not a paraphrase, which would be unwieldy and undesirable, but a short stanza-by-stanza commentary. There is little point, therefore, in reading the next paragraphs unless you have the poem itself to hand.

PART THE FIRST

Stanza 1   The first four lines invoke God, in terms which are appropriate to this poem: he is a master, in power over life and death and notably over the sea. The second four lines refer to the poet's tribulation while resisting conversion. God who put him together almost broke him apart again, 'what with dread'. Now, after the event, still with a shivering uncertainty, the poet traces the kind touch of the forgiving God.

Stanza 2   In that tribulation the poet finally bowed to God's authority. This is the first appearance of the gigantic God of wrath treading down the frail Hopkins—an oppressive image here and in Hopkins's last poems. 'Confess' means 'acknowledge after trying to avoid acknowledging'.

Stanza 3   For a spell, a brief period, the poet was trapped between the gulf of hell and the cruel face of the giant God; but suddenly his heart, with a homing instinct like that of a carrier-pigeon, sensed the kindness of God as revealed in the Host of the Communion service. (The heart obeyed its natural *instress* towards God—see pp. 20-21). I am not sure about the last line; it perhaps means that Hopkins perceived the dual nature of God, and fled from one 'flame'—that of cruelty—to the other—that of gentleness.

Stanza 4   The first four lines deal with the physical 'I': the mortal body, whose sands are always running out. (The description of the sand running is typically exact, an incidental delight for us). The hour-glass is fixed ('fast') to the wall, and the body appears solid and lasting; but within there is constant decay. The second four lines deal with the immortal unchanging 'I'—the soul—kept alive and pure by the streams of God's grace, as the smooth surface of a well is maintained by water from the fells. 'Voel' is a common Welsh word for a hill. Note the subtlety of the word 'vein', which describes vividly the appearance of a stream on a mountain-side, but also refers to Christ's blood, which to a Catholic is the actual redeeming force.

Stanza 5   A hint of Hopkins's theory of inscape. Out of the natural wonder of the world the poet 'wafts' God: that is, he sees God revealed there. The mystery of God in nature must be sensed instinctively by the heart—and it will be more often sensed than fully understood.

Stanza 6   'Stress' may be interpreted as 'the influence of God on man's heart'—the influence for salvation. To appreciate it we should look not to heaven—

Stanza 7 —but to Christ's earthly life and death. 'Going' means living, journeying through life; note that it was a 'womb-life', that is, an ordinary earthly life as distinct from a God-life. 'Grey' perhaps because it was a life of some hardship and grim ending. The 'stress' will be appreciated not by the intellect, but by the heart, at the point when the heart is so oppressed ('hard at bay') that it is forced to recognize the truth. Compare the way the heart finds wings and flies 'to the heart of the Host' when desperate (stanza 3). The last three lines of this stanza powerfully enact the imprisoned truth beating upon the heart; and the realization is an emotional explosion, so that the words are flung into the next stanza.

Stanza 8 It is a sudden, overpowering knowledge which fills the whole being (as when a damson, having been mouthed, bursts in the mouth). It may be an uncomfortable discovery (the taste is bitter-sweet), and men may not have sought it, but they are drawn in spite of themselves to Christ (referred to here in terms of his Crucifixion, which supports the idea of stanza 7, lines 1–5). 'We lash with the best or worst Word last' probably refers to the custom of orators of ending with their most telling point. This is related to the heart's coming out with the truth only at the last moment.

Stanza 9 This stanza is a hymn to God, emphasizing his ferocious might and the kindness which he can show after exercising that might. Here the first mention of wrecking is made. The whole stanza, with its paradoxes of deceptively simple wording, is a key to the poem, or a motto for it.

Stanza 10 The hymn is continued: the poet asks God to convert all men, either by violent revelation, as with Paul on the road to Damascus, or—preferably—by a milder and gradual transformation, as in the case of Saint Augustine. Notice the quasi-musical ending, like the end of a classical first movement

but be adored, but be adored King.

The stress on 'adored' makes it desirable to pause slightly before giving the final 'King'. The end of Part the Second is similar, on a more grandiose scale.

Stanza 11 Death (personified in a medieval manner) is always announcing himself; yet we imagine we are 'rooted in earth'. With scornful irony Hopkins disposes of this in the one ejaculation, 'Dust!', which sums up several apt comments. We are rooted not in a firm earth but in frail mortal flesh, like a plant rooted only in dust. We are only dust ourselves, at first and last. Hopkins continues by using the entirely traditional image of death as a reaper, but gives it a fresh look. 'Wave with the meadow' superbly suggests the foolishly cheerful nodding heads of irreligious mankind. The scythe is 'sour' because it is un-pleasant to us, and also for the onomatopoeia of its partnership with 'scythe', reproducing the hiss of the blade in the meadow. 'Cringe' means here 'strike low'; 'blear' has similar suggestions to those of 'sour', and 'share' means of course the ploughshare.

Stanza 12 The narrative begins. There were two hundred on board—mostly 'not under thy feathers'—not good Catholics; yet perhaps at the last God generously gathered them in (the bay of God's church extended over them, adding their names to the 'rounds' made by the 'reeve' God. Hopkins uses 'reeve' here as a verb). This is an anticipation of the hope raised in stanza 31.

Stanzas 13, 14 and 15 continue a straightforward narrative of great vividness and power, describing the actual shipwreck. 'Whorl' in 14 means 'propeller'; it is obvious why Hopkins preferred it. The opening of 15 offers another personification, of a rather more Victorian kind. In line 5 of this stanza the indefinite article is placed between adjective and noun; there is a note on this kind of construction on page 136, but it is of no immediate importance here, provided the meaning is understood ('a terrible dusk closed down a sad day').

Stanza 16 A sailor descends from the rigging to try to rescue the women below. In spite of the rope's protection, he is dashed to death by the gale; and the rope keeps him in view for hours, bobbing through the blur of foam. It seems very possible that Hopkins invented this detail. In any case, the visualization is masterly, and properly horrific. For 'burl' compare the word 'hurly-burly' (from which Hopkins also takes his special favourite, 'hurl').

Stanza 17 God was behind it all, so it was hopeless to struggle. The hubbub, realistically suggested ('Night roared . . . The woman's wailing, the crying of child without check'), is interrupted by the rising up of the senior nun, to address her fellow-passengers. 'Lioness' for her courage and strength; 'prophetess' because she is to speak of Christ's redemption of Christians and the reward which could lie in store for them; and 'virginal' (it has been suggested) as a pun on her chastity and her musical voice (though a virginal would be of little use in a tempest).

Stanza 18 This is difficult. Hopkins turns on his own heart and addresses it, puzzled by the tears of 'glee' which affect him as he thinks of these events. The 'bower of bone' is the rib-cage; the heart has 'turned for an exquisite smart'—that is, has been moved by a sharp sadness not without beauty. The heart tends often towards sin (though I am not entirely persuaded by this interpretation of 'O unteachably after evil'), but is uttering truth now. The tears seem like a happy song, as if full of the spirit of unageing youth; how can this be?

Stanza 19 A very forceful description of the nun calling above the weather. The excellence of this does not, I think, need demonstrating.

Stanzas 20–23 These stanzas are strictly a *digression* from the narrative. 20 is mostly preoccupied with a play upon the various associations—some good, some bad—which the name 'Deutschland' has for Hopkins. 'Coifèd' refers to the nuns' headdress. The Catholic saint Gertrude and Martin Luther the Protestant were both born in the same town; in the same way good has come from Germany, as well as the evil of Protestantism and the grimness of the present instance of the name. Stanza 21 emphasizes that God, compared here to Orion the hunter, was chasing the nuns out of Germany for his own purposes. At every point he was in control, 'weighing the worth' of every moment. And in the storm heaven lay in wait for the nuns. 'Unchancelling' probably means 'denying the nuns a church, a haven'. Stanzas 22 and 23 are a kind of Metaphysical conceit upon the fact that there were five nuns and also five stigmata (four nail-marks and a lance-hole) in Christ's body on the cross. These stigmata appeared miraculously upon the body of St. Francis, whose order the nuns belong to.

Stanza 24 We return to the narrative, by way of a mention of the poet himself, who was safe in his Welsh college—this highlights the exposure of the nun. As death came she called with gladness upon Christ (note the pun in 'christens').

Stanzas 25–27 For three stanzas of considerable difficulty Hopkins muses as to what she could have meant, what could have been her motives. His first theory is that it is 'love in her of the being as her lover had been': a joy, that is, at being in a position similar to that of Christ at his death. Hopkins quells this theory (perhaps rather unconvincingly) by saying that the men in the boat with Christ on the sea of Gennesareth didn't seem to feel any delight in being in extremities with Christ. The second possibility is that she 'cried for the crown'—that the nun was longing for heaven, and selfishly expecting to get a richer reward for having died painfully. Stanza 26 expands this suggestion by describing possible conceptions of heaven, all, of course, in earthly terms (which are interestingly close to those of Hopkins's subsequent nature-sonnets); but the opening of stanza 27 refutes this theory also. It is drudgery, everyday suffering and weariness, which breeds the pathetic 'asking-for-ease' of a defeated personality—not moments of danger and horror like those of the wreck. Again, the appeal of the Passion is stronger to someone praying quietly on his own; but the nun's thought must have been of another sort, in the frenzy of the storm.

Stanza 28 This is the climax. Hopkins's own heart is now coming 'out with it' (see stanza 8 and the notes above on stanzas 5–7), struggling to grasp the truth, and then all at once perceiving it, in a great rush of words. The truth is God—it was God all the time, guiding the whole storm and the wreck. Having seen this the nun was triumphant, and made her death a glorifying of God. Hopkins's language careers along in exultation, and he employs the imagery of royalty and pageantry which recurs in his poetry to describe God's glory.

Stanza 29 This stanza praises the nun's heart, which saw this truth even in the turmoil of the storm. 'Single eye' is a gospel reference (Matthew, vi, 22); we have today the phrase 'single-minded'. How else could she have interpreted it, except in terms of God? 'Simon Peter' and 'Tarpeian' are ways of saying that the nun's heart was steady as a great rock. (Hopkins blundered mildly with 'Tarpeian', which has the wrong associations for those who know that it was the Roman place of execution).

Stanza 30 A new significance appears: the wreck occurred on the eve of the Feast of the Immaculate Conception of the Virgin Mary, the 'one woman without stain'. Hopkins tells us this by addressing Jesus as a light to the heart (echoing the wording of the previous stanza) and as 'maid's son' (emphasizing the point to be made in this one). 'The night thou hadst glory of this nun' is the language of love-poetry, which Hopkins would not consider inappropriate here; he has already called Christ the nun's 'lover'. The difficult last three lines of this stanza draw a parallel between Mary, who 'conceived' Christ in her body, and the nun, who conceived him in her heart, gave birth to him through throes of the heart, having received his message ('Word'), retained it and passed it on.

Stanza 31 The nun is in heaven now, she is receiving her reward. The poet pities the 'unconfessed'—the non-Catholics or lapsed Catholics, who will now be in hell or purgatory. But in the fifth line he changes his mind. The syntax is more than usually confusing here. The subject is 'the breast of the maiden', 'obey' is the verb, and 'Providence'—with its accompanying epithets—the object. She obeyed the kind message of Providence (God), spoke of Christ's redemption of mankind, and startled the poor sheep back into Christianity. Or rather, *perhaps* she did. It is a fervent hope. If so, then the shipwreck is a harvest for God, reaping precious souls. And it proves God's mercy functioning by means of sternness.

Stanzas 32–34 are a hymn of praise, of admiration. The imagery, appropriately, is of sea and flood. The Yore-flood is the great traditional flood—Noah's flood. 'Past all Grasp God' is an adjectival form—God who is beyond all comprehension. God's sovereignty watches but stays aloof until needed. It can be threatening ('bodes') but it will also remain true for ever ('abides'), and whenever called upon God will come, even to those who seem past hope, those who repent in their last breath—to all these he will come in mercy, 'in the storm of his strides'. Stanza 34 prays that God may 'burn' to the world with fresh brightness, and the last three lines emphasize that although the storm was terrifying, it was a mere 'shower', a mild touch of what God might do and on Doomsday will do.

Stanza 35 Hopkins addresses the nun, and asks her to make special intercession in heaven on behalf of the British, at whose door she was drowned. Britain is no longer a Catholic country, and Hopkins prays that it may become so again, that God may 'easter' in us, and dawn upon our darkness. 'Easter' is a fine coinage, implying the resurrection of truth in Britain. The poem ends in a cascade of grandeur, using epithets of chivalry and romance as well as of religion, piling them up like the heavy chords at the end of a symphony. The paraphrasable meaning is less important here than the emotive associations of the diction, but the last line may be roughly interpreted as: the light in the best of our hearts, the Lord of the best of our thoughts. Notice the intricate alliterative and assonantal pattern.

The energy of the poem is extraordinary. It comes firstly from Hopkins's passionate seriousness, his great anxiety to make this a good poem so that he might justify to himself his resumption of poetry-writing, and secondly from his enthusiasm for the new rhythmic theories which he had worked out and the old assonantal methods he had discovered in ancient Welsh and English poetry. It comes also from the sheer full-bloodedness of his approach. He was young, only thirty-one, when he wrote this poem, and, indeed, throughout his poetry he is never much given to restraint either of diction or of emotion. *The Wreck of the Deutschland* represents the best aspects of a Victorian violence of emotion whose worse side distresses us, as in parts of Dickens, in Tennyson, in Swinburne, and in many nineteenth-century composers. This poem is closer to Tchaikovsky's *1812* overture than to an Ode of Keats. Hopkins was an enthusiast of *The Battle of the Baltic,* by Thomas Campbell, and of stirring patriotic songs in general. This poem is not of that sort, but its emotion is no more restrained, its blood no less red.

But within this energy, there is amazing intricacy also. Look at the movement of the verse in, say, stanza 19. First there are two lines of declamation, cleverly phrased and memorable on their own, then a return of the violent sea-description, running on from line 4 into the strong 'Blinds' at the beginning of line 5. Note the surging insistence, in lines 5 and 6, of—

> But she that weather sees one thing, one;
> Has one fetch in her;

—and then the freer movement of the last two lines as her words 'rode over the storm's brawling'.

Or look at the ironic compression of the word 'Dust!', already noted, in stanza 11; and the word-play throughout the poem, used for serious ends, as in 'Mark, the mark is of man's make' (22) or 'The cross to her she calls Christ to her, christens her wild-worst Best' (24).

The recurrence of the word 'vein' in stanzas 4, 31, and 33; the single stanza of sensuous delight (26) with such phrases as 'Blue-beating and hoary-glow height'; and the remarkable play of sound in stanza 8—lash, lush, plush, flesh, gush, flush, flash— these are representative of the repeated successes of the poem in details as well as in its narrative sweep.

Value-judgments are harder with this than with most poems, because there is nothing to compare it with. But that too is part of Hopkins's achievement. He wanted to write a unique poem, he wanted to 'admire and do otherwise'. Notice that in this, his one large-scale work, he chooses a recent event as his subject. He did not allow his brilliance as a classical scholar to lead him into neo-classical elegy or pastorals as lesser poets (particularly Victorians) have done. His great myths are those of the Bible, and of these he uses the traditional images—the field of men reaped by Death, the flock of sheep gathered and guarded by their shepherd—but he manages to give them an air of newness.

Hopkins never again had the time or the power to write such a poem. His subsequent verse expands many elements of this work, and with greater personal relevance at the time, but it says little that is not said, at least briefly, in the *Deutschland*. *The Loss of the Eurydice* seems like a pathetic attempt to recapture the exceptional inspiration of this work, and his last sonnet, *To R.B.*, laments the absence of such inspiration. But once at least it occurred, and the resulting poem would make Hopkins one of our great poets even if it had been followed by nothing else.

4

The 1877 Sonnets

Hopkins must have been conscious of his own success in *The Wreck of the Deutschland*; and it encouraged him to go on writing. 1876 produced nothing more of importance, but 1877 is his richest single year, since a few months saw the composition of thirteen sonnets (from *God's Grandeur* to *In the Valley of the Elwy* in all editions) dealing with inscape, God, and the natural world.

When Hopkins introduces one or another of these poems in his letters it is as an example of metrical experiment, of Sprung Rhythm (see Chapter Eight). But this can be attributed to humility, and to some timidity. To offer the poems to his friends as metrical experiments was easier than to offer them simply as the earnest and impassioned utterances which they are. To a modern reader none of these sonnets presents any difficulty of rhythm; their rhythms are powerful indeed, but by no means difficult to grasp. We can sight-read the verse of the 1877 sonnets. The diction, syntax, and ideas are more difficult. One should start with some understanding of Hopkins's theory of inscape (expounded on p. 22 of this book). These thirteen sonnets are the fullest description—and dramatization—of inscape in Hopkins's work. Sunrise, stars, spring, men, the sea and the skylark, the kestrel, 'dappled things', harvest, and the Welsh landscape—the beauty and the natural individuality of these are manifestations of God, and they make a pressure of goodness upon the poet's heart, which excites him to an act of praise.

'GOD'S GRANDEUR'

Conceived on 23 February 1877, this is one of Hopkins's strongest and clearest poems. 111 of 126 words are monosyllables; true, this is contrived partly for the sake of deliberate monotony in the second quatrain, but it is more the result of Hopkins's endeavour to employ the colloquial idioms of his time and the Anglo-Saxon strength of the language. The first line— 'The world is charged with the grandeur of God'—could not be more direct, nor more natural to the spoken language of men, and the vitality of the metaphor is at once distinctive. (Compare it with an insensitive student's misquotation—'The world is full of the grandeur of God'. How crucial metaphor, and especially verb-metaphor, is to great poetry!) The second line confirms that the 'charged' is meant to suggest energy, but the word also evokes weight and power (a cavalry charge; charged with a burden). Hopkins told Bridges that 'foil' in the second line meant gold-leaf, tinsel, or tinfoil. Note how he chooses the northern (and today strictly incorrect) form 'shook', not the weaker 'shaken'. The image of 'oil Crushed' is probably that of crushed olives, from which the oil would 'ooze' and 'gather'. The 'Crushed' has obvious force in being a monosyllable carried over from the previous line. 'Reck' is an old word meaning 'heed', 'pay attention to': we still have it in 'reckless', and Hopkins uses it in several other poems.

The first four lines, then, assert God's grandeur; the second four present in contrast the weariness and ugliness of man's works in the world. The double repetition in line 5 is a simple but bold device, and it leads to the dragging internal rhymes of 'seared', 'bleared', 'smeared' in line 6 and the equally heavy rhyme-plus-alliteration of line 7—'wears man's smudge and shares man's smell'. Notice the long vowels in 'seared', 'wears' and their companions, and the intentionally clumsy consonants of ' 's man's smudge' and ' 's man's smell'. The last words of the octet are perhaps a slight weakness, but we should realize the implications, which are—by association with oriental and Old Testament reverence towards holy ground—that the ground on which we walk is holy, being 'charged' with God, and we have lost contact with it.

The sestet opens with a similar colloquial straightforwardness to that of the octet:

>And for all this, nature is never spent,
>There lives the dearest freshness deep down things;

These two lines are in a way the boldest of the whole poem. For all this', 'dearest', 'deep down things' and perhaps even 'spent' are the phrases of casual conversation. A schoolmaster of the time would certainly have censured their use in a schoolboy's essay; and even today 'dearest' dangerously suggests *A Thought for the Day* (or *Week*) in a popular journal. But Hopkins repeatedly takes these risks ('lovely', another magazine epithet, is one of his favourite adjectives), and the force of his individuality, his statement, and the accompanying diction carries them off; so he succeeds in using 'the current language heightened'. The naivety of the phrasing in the lines quoted is, it may be argued, appropriate to the idea of 'freshness'.

The sunset-sunrise progress of lines 11 and 12 is simple but far from dull—the alliterations invite the reader to luxuriate over them—and with the last two lines of the sonnet Hopkins transforms his sestet from a familiar Victorian nature-poem into something approaching religious dogma. The 'Because', coming after the dash at the end of line 12, is intended to be emphatic: the reader is not to be allowed to avoid this conclusion. The world is charged with the grandeur of God, and it is God that causes the constant redemption by nature. Yet although this is a matter of dogma, Hopkins does much to carry it into the least sympathetic mind, by the vividness and sensitivity of his metaphor:

>over the bent
>World broods with warm breast and with ah! bright wings.

Again the alliterative pattern is luxurious, especially in 'broods', 'breast', and 'bright'; and the continuity of 'b' and 'w' holds the sentence closely together in spite of the startling enjambement (startling because the separation of adjective and noun by line-division is almost unprecedented. Perhaps Hopkins intends to picture in this device the great curve of the 'bent' world).

Like all Hopkins's poems, this is a sonnet to be read aloud.

This was begun the day after *God's Grandeur*. The excitement and splendour of the first seven lines, which are an elaborate metaphorical description of starlight, hardly need comment. 'Delves' in line 4 is the plural of 'delf', a mine or pit. 'Whitebeam' is a small tree whose leaves have silvery undersides, and so will show white when 'windbeat'; 'abeles' are White Poplars, which again have white undersides to the leaves. 'Flake-doves' suggest the snow-whiteness of doves and also, perhaps, their appearance as they fly away at 'a farmyard scare.'

Line 8 breaks away from this excitement to make the more rational remark which is necessary if the poem is to be more than an indulgent sketch. All this loveliness is something for which we must pay before it is really ours (or its true significance is seen). The ninth line continues this sober thought: 'Buy then! bid then!—What?—Prayer, patience, alms, vows'. What should I bid with? man asks, and the answer is: with acts of reverence and devotion.

Lines 10 and 11 are a return to the metaphorical description of the stars. They are like blossom, in May on apple-trees, in March on 'sallows' (pussy-willow) whose blossom is covered in yellow meal (compare 'meal-drift' in *Hurrahing in Harvest*). This is, in traditional terms, a weakness in the structure of the sonnet—the lines are padding-out the sestet with material belonging to the already rather repetitive octet. But I doubt if any reader senses weakness here; rather one would say that Hopkins has cleverly broken the rules in order to maintain the insistent excitement.

In the last three lines the exclamation marks cease, and calm transforms the previous uninterpreted excitement. These stars shelter and enclose Christ, as a barn encloses rich harvest. 'Shocks' are sheaves of corn; 'house' is a verb meaning 'find a house for themselves' ('shocks' is the subject); 'withindoors' is an adverb meaning 'indoors'. The paling—the door or frame of the barn—is 'piece-bright', studded with stars, and it 'shuts home' (guards) Christ the husband (he is wedded to all mankind). And not only Christ, but also his mother Mary and all his saints. In other words, as in *Deutschland* 5, 'he is under the world's splendour and wonder'; the stars are one way in which, as in *God's Grandeur*, the charge of God will 'flame out, like shining from shook foil'.

'SPRING'

This poem, written in May 1877, is one of Hopkins's clearest, and will not be examined in detail here. Excellences to be noted are the direct colloquial opening, the conscious melody of alliterations and assonances and the clear interpretation in the sestet of what the octet describes. Spring, the poet says, is an echo of primal innocence, in Eden; so is spring in human life, that is, the innocence of children, which Hopkins prays God may secure for himself before it is corrupted. The last line reminds us that Christ himself was the child of innocence, of a 'maid'. In later years Hopkins wrote several poems about the instinctive goodness of children or simple adults he met, and images of May, or spring-time, are always among his favourites. In *Deutschland* 26, 'the heaven of desire' is described in terms of 'pied and peeled May', and the bitter late sonnet *Thou art indeed just, Lord . . .* contrasts the surge of spring with the poet's sterility.

'THE LANTERN OUT OF DOORS'

Though produced in the same month as *Spring*, this is a less happy poem. It even anticipates slightly the frustration of Hopkins's late sonnets. Men pass the poet by, some of whom are exceptional people in one way or another, and he cannot make lasting contact with them. 'Wind What most I may eye after' is a tortuous way of saying 'however much I try to follow them with my eye' (and doubtless this stands for other ways of keeping in touch, by correspondence or by news from others); always he loses contact, and cannot 'be in at the end'.

Ostensibly this is the distress of a priest, wishing to keep in touch with and exercise a pastoral influence over people, and the last three lines are the resolution of this distress: Christ is always watching over them, he has ransomed them on the Cross, he is their 'first, fast, last friend'. But it is hard not to feel that the poem is unconsciously a statement of the poet's own loneliness, and his need for contact with men 'whom either beauty bright In mould or mind or what not else makes rare'.

This sonnet is also of May 1877. It contrasts the 'nature' of sea and skylark with the ugliness of a man-made city in the full aftermath of the Industrial Revolution. As always, the octet describing natural beauty is finely done, especially the sound of the sea in—'With a flood or a fall, low lull-off or all roar'.

The second quatrain is explained at great length by Hopkins in a letter to Bridges, which is quoted in the notes to most editions. The general sense is that the lark's song sounds as free and fresh as silk running off a reel, the reel descending as it unwinds. The sestet is unusually depressed for Hopkins at this period, and closer, perhaps, to the conventional Victorian poem. Coming so soon after *Spring*, the account of man's origin as 'first slime' seems an unfair loading of the balances, and I doubt if Hopkins could keep to this grim view of mankind when he ceased to generalize. His poems and remarks about individual people are full of the sense of their nobility.

'THE WINDHOVER'

With this sonnet (conceived 30 May 1877) Hopkins returns to the ecstasy of the first two sonnets and of the *Deutschland*. It is his boldest attempt so far, and in 1879 he described it as 'the best thing I ever wrote'.

It is useful to relate the sonnet to the others already discussed. The basic structure is the same: the octet describes the kestrel, and the poet's excited joy at its flight, and the sestet describes and interprets the inscape of this experience. Lines 13 and 14 of *God's Grandeur*, 12–14 of *The Starlight Night*, and 8–10 of *Spring* correspond, in their religious interpretation of the experience, to the sestet of *The Windhover*, which is, however, rather less explicit and much more dramatic.

'Caught' in line 1 means 'caught a sight of'. The early images are of a royal court; the bird is the 'minion', or favourite, of morning, and the 'dauphin' or heir-apparent of the 'kingdom of daylight'. He is 'drawn' out by the 'dapple-dawn'. He rides the air and in his strength makes the air seem to roll 'level underneath him steady', a huge adjectival phrase. 'Rung upon the rein' is a description of the bird turning, canting with one wing dipped and one up. The metaphor is from the breaking-in of horses, who are first made to trot round in a circle, held on a leading rein by a man in the middle.

'Wimpling' is applied to the feathers or muscles of the wing in its supple movement—overlapping in pleats like an ironed and starched wimple. The next 'swing' of the bird is compared to the smooth sweeping of an ice-skate round a bow-shaped bend; but the following words emphasize also the might of this movement, against 'the big wind'. 'In hiding' is presumably to be taken literally: the poet was in a hide, or at least standing out of sight. (Some critics, however, have seen in these words a complex sense of guilt at enjoyment). 'Achieve' means 'achievement'.

Here Hopkins's rhythmic skill is breathtaking, and no theory of Sprung Rhythm explains it fully. First, notice the strong enjambements throughout the first eight lines. Hopkins is always generous with enjambement, but here the propelling force from one line into another (especially at the end of line 1) is particularly fierce. The flight, throughout the first seven lines, is unflagging, though two distinct stages are described (one in each quatrain). What most strikes the poet, and is most emphasized, is the *ease* of the bird's movement, not flapping or faltering against the wind. The three strong participles 'riding', 'striding', and 'gliding' present this for us, supported by the very expansiveness of the first three lines.

This power is summed up in the image of the skate, and again in the use of 'gliding' in this sentence: 'the hurl and gliding Rebuffed the big wind.' 'Hurl' suggests extreme violence or force; 'rebuffed' and 'big' with their common consonant, suggest effort; 'gliding' is the exact antithesis. The power and effort are there, but such is 'the mastery of the thing' that it is under perfect control.

Returning to the rhythm, note line 5, the shortest in the poem because of its consecutive stresses, with the hiatus (small sharp break) between the two 'off's as the bird begins a fresh movement. Perhaps this is one single flap of the wings.

The sestet opens *fortissimo*, with two stresses, alliteration and a common vowel: 'Brúte beáuty'. The two words have opposite connotations (Beauty and the Beast, even?), and so in this phrase is condensed much of the point of the poem. The word 'thing' at the end of the octet is not a weak vagueness chosen for the rhyme; Hopkins is exclaiming at the realization that something mortal and animal should show such mastery. Line 9 as a whole is an extraordinary line. The whole experience is being summoned, and in the word 'Buckle!' (line 10) being *fastened* together into the single experience of inscape. An alternative, more specifically Christian, interpretation is that 'buckle' means 'collapse': the bird is most fully itself when it falls, as Christ was in his sacrifice, out of which came the 'fire' of resurrection. More puzzling is the capitalization of the word 'AND'—a device which Hopkins never repeats; probably it is simply to ensure emphasis. In conversation we may say *'And*, by Jove, you should have seen what happened then. . . .'

'Thee', since the poem is subtitled *To Christ Our Lord*, is a direct address to Christ. Again God's grandeur is flaming out, this time in the bird's majesty; and this grandeur is 'a billion Times told lovelier, more dangerous' even than that majesty. 'Dangerous' is a curious word; but a later sonnet offers some help, the one beginning, 'To what serves mortal beauty—dangerous;' and concluding that mortal ('brute') beauty must not be excessively cherished (see also the discussion of *The Leaden Echo and the Golden Echo* on pp. 89–90). In Chapter One Hopkins's sense of the danger of too much devotion to mortal beauty was noted; that theme underlies this poem in particular. God's grandeur, we are told now, is far *more* dangerous, which perhaps suggests both 'more seductive' and 'more to be feared'. And God is also Hopkins's hero, his 'chevalier' (compare the heroic and chivalric imagery which occurs in the *Deutschland*). These difficult three lines form a violent emotional climax, similar to that of the 28th stanza of the *Deutschland*. Hopkins attempts to generate an ultimate in excitement because he is recording an ultimate in experience. This *is* God, too bright to be looked at, flaming out; it is the 'anvil-ding' which converted Saul, the 'great voice, as of a trumpet' which brought Revelation to St. John the Divine. In the verse the experience is enacted—one hears the poet gasp.

The last three lines are a kind of aftermath, but of great importance. More calmly, they emphasize that this is not a unique experience but one readily available, if one is ready to see God revealed wherever one looks. Two examples are given, intended to be more humdrum than the kestrel: the glint of the ploughshare turning a furrow ('sillion'), and the sudden new colours of coals breaking in the fire. In the second image there are suggestions of consolation after drudgery ('blue-bleak' becoming 'gold-vermilion'—again royal) and of glory through pain ('gall themselves, and gash. . .') which are personally important to Hopkins, as well as typically Victorian. 'Ah my dear', apparently having erotic associations which might seem blasphemous, is in fact remembered from George Herbert's *Love*, where it is addressed (as here) to God.

'PIED BEAUTY'

This poem does not appear to be a sonnet, but Hopkins called it a Curtal Sonnet, being a specially devised form (see p. 123). The quietness of this poem, and the tendency of the anthologizers to make it represent the poet too frequently, especially in anthologies compiled for children, may put some readers off. But it is original in a way typical of Hopkins, and in the simplicity is a dignity which does not cloy. Its significance among the other sonnets of 1877 is in the emphasis it places upon individuality, the special characteristics of things—rose-moles on trout, the gear of different trades, 'All things counter, original, spare, strange'. This distinctive quality of things is an aspect of inscape; Hopkins called it the 'sakes' of a thing, and strove always to capture it. In this respect *Pied Beauty* can be linked with the 'kingfishers' sonnet, No. 57 in *Poems*.

HURRAHING IN HARVEST'

This sonnet, written 1 September 1877, varies the pattern of

'Beech, Godshill Church behind. Fr. Appledurcombe'. Drawing by the poet,
25 July (?) 1865

Harry Ploughman

Hard as hurdle arms, with a broth of goldish flue
Breathed round; the rack of ribs; the scooped flank;
      lank
Rope-over thigh; knee-bank; and barrelled shank—
      Head and foot, shoulder and shank,
By a grey eye's heed steered well, one crew, fall to;
Stand at stress. Each limb's barrowy brawned thew
That onewhere curded, onewhere sucked or sank —
      Soared or sank —,
Though as a beechbole firm, finds his, as at a rollcall,
      rank
And features, in flesh, what deed he each must do —
      His sinew-service where do.

He leans to it, Harry bends, look. Back, elbow, and
      liquid waist
In him, all quail to the wallowing o' the plough. 'S
      cheek crimsons; curls
Wag or crossbridle, in a wind lifted, windlaced —
      See his wind- lilylocks -laced;
Churlsgrace, too, child of Amansstrength, how it
      hangs or hurls
Them—broad in bluff hide his frowning feet lashed!
      raced
With, along them, cragiron under and cold furls—
      With a wet-fire-flushed furls.

Dromore Sept. 1887

marks used:

(1) ∧ strong stress; which does not differ much from

(2) ⌒ pause or dwell on a syllable, which need not however have the metrical stress;

(3) ′ the metrical stress, marked in doubtful cases only;

(4) ⌄ quiver or circumflexion, making one syllable nearly two, most used with diphthongs and liquids;

(5) ⌢ between syllables slurs them into one;

(6) ‿ over three or more syllables gives them the time of ~~two~~ one half foot

(7) ⌣ ~~under a~~ ~~syllable or more~~ the outside; under one or more syllables make them extrametrical: a slight pause follows as if the voice were silently making its way back to the highroad of the verse

Left: Hopkins's handwritten copy of *Harry Ploughman* and *above:* the metrical markings employed in the poem

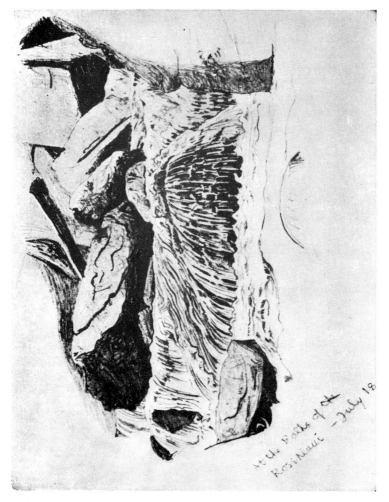

'At the Baths of Rosenlaui'. Drawing by the poet. 18 July 1868

thought slightly from that of the inscape-sonnets so far discussed, and it presents also an extension of statement about inscape. The first four lines describe what would before have been done in seven or eight: the scene, stooks in a field and clouds above. 'Barbarous' suggests both 'wild' and 'bearded' (the ears of corn). Lines 3 and 4 have an almost playful tone, in 'wilder, wilful-wavier Meal-drift moulded ever. . .' Rather than 'shaped', 'moulded' probably means 'gone mouldy'—Hopkins compares the fluffy white of clouds to fluffy white of mould on meal. It is typical of the poet that he should not squeamishly recoil from mould, but be pleased by it and use it to describe the clouds he liked. Compare his delight in 'weeds' in *Spring*.

The second quatrain describes the poet 'gleaning' God from the skies (compare 'wafting him out of it' in *Deutschland* 5) and God's reply through all aspects of the scene. Note the progressive excitement of rhythm—

> I walk, I lift up, I lift up heart, eyes,
> Down all that glory in the heavens to glean our Saviour . . .

—and the contradiction of 'up' and 'Down'. The picture is of the poet throwing his head back and then gazing all over the sky down to the horizon.

The first two lines of the sestet emphasize the point, that God is in everything. 'Hung' superbly suggests the poised stillness of hills in the distance; 'world-wielding shoulder' again suggests the giant-God of the *Deutschland*, and a related antithesis is made in line 9:

> Majestic—as a stallion stalwart, very-violet-sweet!

(Compare stanza 9 of the *Deutschland*).

The enjambement 'shoulder Majestic' suggests hugeness, the single phrase easily spanning two lines. In line 11, however, there is a new development of thought, an explicit statement of something absent in the earlier poems. The landscape was here and 'but the beholder wanting' (that is, missing); now that poet and landscape come together, the joy generated makes a great act of praise for God. The heart opens its wings ('rears' suggests a large, powerful bird, so a powerful emotion) and 'half hurls earth for him off under his feet'. 'Him' must be the beholder, but there is a hint of 'for God' also. This coming-together is the same as the 'buckling' together of 'Brute beauty and valour and act, oh, air, pride, plume' in *The Windhover*.

'THE CAGED SKYLARK'

Also of September 1877, this is a metaphorical meditation upon man's body and soul. Lacking the urgent inspiration of the earlier sonnets, it seems somewhat stillborn. The cage, or prison, is man's body when its needs or weaknesses become too oppressive—"in drudgery, day-labouring-out life's age'. The body, however, need not be like this, and indeed the soul could not exist without the body as a house, or 'nest':

> Man's spirit will be flesh-bound when found at best,
> But uncumbered:

The 'risen' man is no more encumbered by his body ('bones') than a meadow is encumbered by the touch of a rainbow. The reference is to the Resurrection: the best state will be when man's spirit is bound to the risen flesh (after the Resurrection of the body).

'IN THE VALLEY OF THE ELWY'

This poem is constructed in such a way that it is very easily misunderstood. The octet describes 'a house where all were good To me'; the first three lines of the sestet describe Wales. It is natural (given the title also) to assume that this house is in Wales, in fact in the valley of the Elwy. Not so. Hopkins explained it to Bridges thus:

> The frame of the sonnet is a rule of three sum *wrong*, thus: As the sweet smell to those kind people so the Welsh landscape is NOT to the Welsh; and then the author and principle of all 4 terms is asked to bring the sum right.

Unfortunately Hopkins doesn't point the contrast sufficiently in the poem, which flaws it seriously.

The first quatrain describes the house he liked. The first two lines skilfully combine three separate statements, each of which survives in essence, as in a Cubist painting: 'I remember a house where all were good'; 'all were good to me'; and 'I deserved no such thing'. Note also the easy use of the colloquialism 'God knows'; Hopkins means it literally.

The second quatrain says that the house and its people were matched by and fitted with the air about them; the air seemed to hood them like a sheltering wing, and all this seemed inevitable and right. There was a consistency of goodness.

The sestet, written in end-stopped lines of unusual calm, starts by contrasting the goodness of the *Welsh* air, in the valley of the Elwy this time, with 'the inmate'—the Welsh people, whom Hopkins apparently did not find 'lovely'. The particular cause of his dissatisfaction is not stated; probably it is simply that the Welsh are not Catholics. The last three lines ask God to bring the Welsh people round to a goodness which will fit that of the landscape. God is described in terms which have previously occurred in the *Deutschland*.

The least of these sonnets is a distinctive and memorable poem. Taken together, they make a sustained expression of the goodness of life and God, which is great Romantic poetry. Thirteen poems is not many, but some of their distinction is in their rareness. Like all Hopkins's best work, they are created in tension. Several of them seem to blaze with an inspiration of uncomfortable urgency. Hopkins was not again to be visited with such powerful inspiration until he went to Ireland in 1884, and then it was in very brief spells, and sprang from a very different psychological condition. Knowing this we more fully appreciate the poems of this one, happier year.

5

Poems 1878–1883

After being ordained priest on 23 September 1877, Hopkins apparently found himself too busy to write poetry. 1878 produced only two poems, *The May Magnificat*, a 'popular' piece written to be hung with others, anonymously, in the college at Stonyhurst, and *The Loss of the Eurydice*. The former is perhaps the better poem, but is clearly of a minor kind, whereas the *Eurydice* is an earnest attempt to write a sequel to the *Deutschland* and to experiment further in rhythm and rhyme.

Both poems are in four-line stanzas, rhyming *aabb*; the stress pattern in *The May Magnificat* is 4:4:3:3, and in the *Eurydice* 4:4:3:4. The short, neat stanza is entirely appropriate to the lighter piece; there is an expected balance and regularity about the lines, which Hopkins presumably supplied in order to please his less literary brothers. As in the *Deutschland*, the Sprung Rhythm is there but can always be read at sight, and enjambement, though frequent, is never too violent; there is time for a brief pause at the end of each line.

Perhaps it is the violent enjambements of *The Loss of the Eurydice*, coupled with rhymes that seem almost deliberately provocative, that spoils the poem for some readers.

> For did she pride her, freighted *fully, on*
> Bounden bales or a hoard of *bullion?*
>
> . . . But what black Boreas *wrecked her? he*
> Came equipped, deadly-el*ectric.* . . .

In this poem Hopkins, who once wrote to Bridges that he could never abide a bad rhyme, offers us: 'all un-'/'fallen', 'aerial'/'burial', 'seamen'/'be men', 'wrought her'/'water', 'England'/'mingle and', 'with her'/'thither', and 'portholes'/ 'mortals' in the first ten stanzas alone. In spite of the poet's instructions that the poem should be read 'with the ears', it is above all the *listener* that these lines offend.

This, however, is a superficial awkwardness, and there are strange rhymes in other Hopkins poems, which nevertheless succeed. The real stiltedness of the *Eurydice* comes, perhaps, from the shortness of the stanza adopted, with the closeness (risking jingle) of the rhymes. Statement is very compressed, as in the first four lines of the *Deutschland* stanza, and there is no opportunity for the richer, fuller expression of the second four lines which that stanza offers. Compare the account of the wreck in the *Deutschland* with stanza 9 of the *Eurydice*:

> Too proud, too proud, what a press she bore!
> Royal, and all her royals wore.
> Sharp with her, shorten sail!
> Too late; lost; gone with the gale.

Again, there is in the first half of the poem a strange vulgarity, in the rhymes quoted, in the tendency towards jingle ('And you were a liar, O blue March day. Bright sun lanced fire in the heavenly bay'), and in the apparent coarseness of

> Death teeming in by her portholes
> Raced down decks, round messes of mortals.   11

or in the self-parody of

> would follow
> His charge through the champ-white water-in-a-wallow ...   12

Perhaps it is linked to Hopkins's enthusiasm for patriotic songs:

> Sydney Fletcher, Bristol-bred,
> (Low lie his mates now on watery bed)   15

Every inch a tar,
Of the best we boast our sailors are.   19

The later part of the poem, where narrative gives way to
meditation, has a much surer dignity. The short stanza lends
itself better to this calmer statement and to epigrammatic balance.
Having described the loss of the *Eurydice*, a training-ship whose
crew was therefore particularly young, and 'precious passing
measure', Hopkins dwells a moment on one particular corpse, to
emphasize the lost potential.

O his nimble finger, his gnarled grip!
Leagues, leagues of seamanship
    Slumber in these forsaken
Bones, this sinew, and will not waken.   21

Here the rhythm is characteristic of Hopkins, but the diction
is traditional (though not hackneyed), and the impression is at
once of a greater firmness than in earlier, more verbally sensational stanzas.

The poet relates the loss of these lives to the loss of so many
English souls (stanzas 22–26). He could let the past be, he says,
forgive the desecration of Catholic shrines, but the loss of the
souls of these men he must 'deplore', and wonder 'why my
master bore it' (England, in its pre-Reformation days, having
once been one of Christ's strongholds). In stanza 26 he assures
himself that some time God will again redeem the country:

but let be, let be:
More, more than was will yet be.

The last four stanzas consider the grief of mothers and lovers
bereaved. They are right to weep (stanza 27), but should also
pray to God, not (stanza 30) because there is any hope of
redemption from hell, but because for souls 'sunk in seeming
fresh' (recently, or young), prayer, at any time until Doomsday,
may fetch eternal pity. The wording, like much of this poem, is
tortuous.

The poems which follow frequently resemble the *Eurydice* in an uneasiness of mood, diction, or syntax. Every poem of Hopkins's maturity has its good moments, but many, in this middle period, are flawed by one or another kind of awkwardness. This is not to say that they are not of distinction and interest; most of them are. One result, perhaps, of the lessened force of the poet's inspiration during this period is a clearer working-out of his theories (rather than his emotions), and several of these poems illuminate Hopkins's ideas throughout his work. There is also a new concern with individuals. The earlier and later poems are generalized or non-human in their subject-matter (or else are about the poet himself), but here Hopkins sets down the 'Jessy or Jack' he encountered in his pastoral work, and the compassionate love he felt for them amidst all the drudgery.

These poems will be taken not always chronologically, but sometimes as their ideas associate them. The first is *Binsey Poplars*, which refers to the felling of real poplars which Hopkins saw on one of his Oxford walks. (A postscript in a letter to Dixon reads: 'March 13 [1879]—I have been up to Godstow this afternoon. I am sorry to say that the aspens that line the river are everyone felled.')

The indentations on the page indicate the number of stresses intended for each line; for example the first three lines have 5 stresses, the fourth 4, the eighth 6 (or perhaps 7). The poem is like a short and free song, the ending in particular suggesting echo or refrain. Its expression is vivid and unforced (an exception perhaps is 'sandalled' in line 6, which is a puzzle, but could perhaps refer to the fragrance of sandalwood, or else to the pattern effect of interlacing straps in a sandal), and it has one image of alarming nervous precision:

> That, like this sleek and seeing ball
> But a prick will make no eye at all, . . .

which anticipates the images of suffering and torture in Hopkins's late work. This poem, like *Henry Purcell* and *Poems* No. 57, turns particularly on the idea of the 'self' of a thing (see Chapter One, pp. 20–22), the essence of inscape. The poet is here distressed at the killing of an individuality. There was a scene here, which now is completely destroyed—the 'self' has been taken out of it, and it is no longer 'especial'; it no longer has what Duns Scotus called *haecceitas*—Thisness.

The theory of self, Thisness, in inscape is defined very clearly in the untitled sonnet *As kingfishers catch fire, dragonflies draw flame . . . (Poems* No. 57). Here the octet deals with 'nature', the sestet with mankind. In both it is the individual quality which God values and for which the thing was made. The distinctive colourings of kingfisher and dragonfly (the clauses describing them have their own private alliterative pattern), the special sound (and circles on the surface—both are implied in 'ring') of stones dropped into wells, the separate note of each string in a musical instrument, or each bell in a peal—each mortal thing reveals in some such way its own uniqueness. Now, as to man, 'the just man' (that is, man who is doing his part in life properly) is just, keeps grace, and in turn makes all he does graceful. This is how man should be, this is how he reveals the true quality of God in himself. Christ 'plays' (like a fountain) in many places, showing the special beauty of a person to God. The last phrase of the poem, 'through the features of men's faces', emphasizes the essential point of the poem, that it is the individual *features* which reveal inscape. In *Henry Purcell* (and *Deutschland* 22) the word for these distinguishing features is 'sakes'.

This 'kingfishers' poem is perhaps Hopkins's best sonnet between *The Windhover* and *Spelt from Sybil's Leaves*. The brilliance of the first line, the clarity of the whole poem, with balance of phrase and alliteration (especially in the sestet) recall *God's Grandeur* or *Spring*. The motive behind the poem is doctrinal rather than emotional, but the poet's senses are very alive and the verse is shaped with that restraint and decorum which we occasionally miss in Hopkins. The image 'Christ plays in ten thousand places' seems to me one of this poet's most effective.

Henry Purcell is another sonnet, regular in rhyme-scheme but puzzling in syntax. The reader may be referred to Hopkins's own explanatory note on the poem, in the *Letters to Robert Bridges* pp. 170–1 (reprinted by most editors in their notes). The first four lines are a prayer that Purcell may have died a good death and so, in view of his good life, have been redeemed in spite of his Protestant religion. The second quatrain makes clear Hopkins's admiration for Purcell. In his music he finds an individuality entirely distinctive and interesting:

> It is the forgèd feature finds me; it is the rehearsal
> Of own, of abrupt self there so thrusts on, so throngs the ear.

'Abrupt' here perhaps means direct, without qualifications or compromises.

The sestet is really a continuation of this idea, but using a new, chief metaphor. Purcell's individuality ('abrupt self') appears constantly, although it is not the composer's own concern to make it appear. The composer is out to express an emotion or an idea, and only incidentally reveals his own distinctiveness. Hopkins submits to the composer's intention ('Let him oh! with his air of angels then lift me, lay me!'), but also makes his own observation of the composer's special character. The metaphor is of a storm-fowl who takes off from a beach with a flap of its wings; all the bird cares about, or 'means', is motion, but the glimpse it gives of its special markings startles and delights us ('fans fresh our wits with wonder').

The awkwardness of the octet, with its inversions and strange rhymes, and a certain flashiness about the sestet, especially in the line, 'The thunder-purple seabeach plumed purple-of-thunder', detract from the sonnet's total achievement; but it remains a memorable and completely original poem, which describes inscape in art rather than in a living thing.

Duns Scotus himself, the philosopher from whom Hopkins drew the theory of inscape, is celebrated in the sonnet *Duns Scotus's Oxford*. The octet describes Oxford, pastoral and urban; the sestet expresses the poet's reverence for the city because it was where Scotus lived, 'he . . . who of all men most sways my spirits to peace'. Scotus was 'of realty the rarest-veined un-raveller', that is, the man who explored most subtly and delicately the nature of reality. The poem ends, uncomfortably for most readers, on a stubborn reference to history and dogma, and with the dull thud of 'Mary without spot' (that is, immaculate). It is of interest, however, not only for its testimony to Scotus's influence on Hopkins or the poet's love of Oxford, but for the words 'sways my spirits to peace', which imply some weariness or struggle. Here the poet's private experience, a sombre acceptance of heavy duties after the early joys of conversion and study, makes an appearance.

Peace, a Curtal Sonnet (see p. 123) written in 1879, voices the distress openly, though by comparison with Hopkins's late sonnets this is still ultimately resolved and 'peaceful'. The poem is so neat and pious and uses so traditionally soothing an image (the wooddove roaming and then settling 'to brood and sit') that it may be felt to be sentimental. But there is a notable integrity about it:

> I'll not play hypocrite
> To own my [my own] heart: I yield you do come sometimes . . .

—and a sense of humour:

> That piecemeal peace is poor peace . . .

—and, as is usual in Hopkins, there is a vivid life in the key-words:

> Patience exquisite,
> That *plumes* to Peace thereafter.

In *Andromeda* Hopkins endeavoured, as he wrote in a letter, 'at a more Miltonic plainness and severity than I have anywhere else'. It is his most impersonal poem, and perhaps for that reason a failure. Andromeda is the Catholic church, threatened by Western enemies; Perseus is Christ. It is, in the worst sense, an academic poem (as the reference to Milton might suggest).

Although the diction and subject are, one supposes, those of Hopkins, the ponderous use of a pagan myth to comment on contemporary matters is typical of bad Victorian poetry. Among Hopkins's work this is bound to seem uninspired and un-inspiring.

Inversnaid is well-known as an easy introduction to Hopkins. It is a straightforward and very vivid description of 'wild nature', with a cry for its preservation. It is interesting to compare the finished last stanza—which although slightly sing-songy hardly lets the poem down—with what appears to be an early draft, in a letter to Bridges (22 February 1879):

> And wander in the wilderness;
> In the weedy wilderness,
> Wander in the wilderness.

This is evidence, if we needed it, that Hopkins was no more a poet of first thoughts, and no less a determined craftsman, than other great poets. The rhythm in the finished version is altogether firmer and more vigorous.

The Blessed Virgin Compared to the Air We Breathe was written, like *The May Magnificat*, for public consumption when hung up amongst others at Stonyhurst. Only the length and verse-form (three-stress couplets) are untypical of Hopkins. The extended composition is handled with a confident cleverness characteristic (like the poem's basic image) of the Metaphysical poets of the seventeenth century (whom he admired), but this kind of intricate image-association occurs elsewhere in Hopkins (e.g. in *The Caged Skylark*, *The Sea and the Skylark*, or in stanzas 22 and 23 of the *Deutschland*). For non-Catholics this is a difficult poem, but we can admire the expression at many points, and in particular the Blake-like simplicity with which Hopkins makes the basic statements.

> Through her we may see him
> Made sweeter, not made dim,
> And her hand leaves his light

Sifted to suit our sight.
Be thou then, O thou dear
Mother, my atmosphere. . . .

The same simplicity of expression is intended in *Spring and Fall*, a short poem in four-stress couplets addressed 'to a young child'. This is a well-known piece, popular perhaps by reason of a certain knowing sentimentality which mars the poem by comparison with Hopkins's best. Margaret weeps over the fallen leaves of Goldengrove, and the poet tells her she is weeping, without knowing it, for the passing of all mortal things, including herself. This is so empty of Hopkins's resolute faith in immortal qualities that it is bound to seem an exercise in mannered simplicity, more characteristic, at heart, of the Victorian age than of the poet. The natural foil to this poem is the intense and full-blooded *That Nature is a Heraclitean Fire and of the comfort of the Resurrection*.

Ribblesdale is a somewhat laborious sonnet which seems to try to recapture the spirit of the 1877 sonnets. Earth, the natural world, has no means of pleading its beauty with God except its mere existence, which is enough. Man, who ought to be earth's 'eye, tongue, or heart', is self-obsessed, and mars both this world and his chances of the world to come. At this, Earth is bound to be distressed. It is a strangely lifeless poem, lacking the colloquial ease which vitalizes most of Hopkins's work.

With one exception, the remaining poems of this period deal with people: four about individuals the poet knew in his capacity as priest, and one which is more about himself and his attitude towards himself and others. This last, *The Candle Indoors,* thus anticipates to some extent the late sonnets, though it is a fairly calm poem. In the first four lines the poet watches the light of a candle in a cottage window as he is out walking. The fourth line refers to the rays of light, seeming to go forward and back and to be parallel like tramlines. In the second quatrain he wonders who is within, and in an earnest curiosity prays they are Godly people. Hopkins slips easily into fragments of dialect:

> a-wanting, just for lack
> Of answer the eagerer a-wanting Jessy or Jack
> There God to aggrandise, God to glorify.

After 'There' a pause is necessary, to link the word to the previous phrase, not the subsequent. This is a slight clumsiness.

In the sestet Hopkins turns upon himself, with a robust colloquialism:

> Come you indoors, come home. . . .

He is outside, being called in; or, more important, he is troubling himself about other people's morality, when he is far from perfect himself. The last three lines use traditional metaphors from the gospels, but with a Hopkinsian ring to them. It is a vigorous and scornful conclusion, unique to Hopkins (one cannot imagine him being scornful towards others).

Lancashire, and its dialect, are even more in evidence in *Felix Randal*, one of Hopkins's best-liked poems. Felix Randal the blacksmith is dead, after a long illness (Hopkins says it was four fatal disorders at once) during which his strong body wasted and at times he lost his reason. The second quatrain describes how Felix Randal reconciled himself at last to his illness, with fortitude, and how Hopkins had heard his confession ('tendered . . . our sweet reprieve and ransom . . . to him'). The poet prays that Randal's sins may be forgiven. This is worded in Lancashire colloquialisms which help him to avoid stale piety:

> Ah well, God rest him all road ever he offended!

The first three lines of the sestet link poet and farrier more closely. Hopkins's visits to the sick man had started a real affection, and he viewed Randal's increasing calm of mind with a tender pride, because he had helped the sick man towards it:

> My tongue had taught thee comfort, touch had quenched thy
>   tears . . .

This was a considerable achievement, says Hopkins in the last three lines, because formerly Randal had been a 'boisterous' character. 'How far from then forethought of' means 'no one in those days would have anticipated this calm and these tears in a man like you'. 'Random' means 'built of rough stone'. 'Fettle' means 'beat into shape, put in order'.

It is a poem of strength, especially in the first four and the last three lines. The very grandeur of the ending suggests a slight ambivalence in Hopkins's attitude. Primarily he is giving thanks that the man was converted and made patient, and that he (Hopkins) should have been the agent of this conversion. But the poem also grieves for the passing of one who was so much alive, 'big-boned and hardy-handsome', and the last lines suggest that it is this earlier, unconverted, violent (but 'boisterous' implies sympathy on the writer's part) picture which he most warmly retains:

> When thou at the random grim forge, powerful amidst peers,
> Didst fettle for the great gray drayhorse his bright and battering
>   sandal!

A similar affection appears in three poems about boys Hopkins met in the course of his duties. Probably the hypersensitive poet, with his nervous enthusiasms and spurts of irreverent humour, was as a priest a greater success with children than with the coarsened adults he so often encountered. The story of *The Handsome Heart* is of interest:

> . . . two boys of our congregation gave me much help in the sacristy in Holy Week. I offered them money for their services, which the elder refused, but being pressed consented to take it laid out in a book. The younger followed suit; then when some days after I asked him what I shd. buy answered as in the sonnet. ['Father, what you buy me I like best'.] His father is Italian and therefore sells ices.
>
> To Bridges, 14 August 1879

The poem, with such a title and such a subject, runs the

gravest risks of sentimentality. (Hopkins's own comment is 'I thought it not very good'. Bridges, not a good critic of his friend's work, had singled it out for special praise.) The second quatrain says the story shows the good instinct of the heart, which is easily and naturally gracious when doing 'its own fine function, wild and self-instressed'. The metaphor used is the same as that of *Deutschland* 3: the homing pigeon. Left like this the poem would be excessively optimistic and sweet, but the sestet, while praising the boy highly, recognizes that it is 'in this case', not in all cases, and that he may yet waver from the good path. The last three lines wonder what prayer the poet should pray for the child, to whom everything seems already granted. The answer is to pray that he may so continue, running all the race of life on this course and with an even firmer devotion. The sobriety of this saves the poem from glibness.

The same prayer, for the same motives, ends *The Bugler's First Communion*, a longer, unorthodox poem written in stanzas of four longish lines (stresses 5, 5, 3, 5) with much inversion, enjambement, and feminine (two-syllable) rhyme. 'A bugler boy from barrack . . . over the hill There' asked the priest to officiate at his First Communion. As in *Felix Randal* and *The Handsome Heart* Hopkins feels a certain justified pride in having so won the boy's affection in the cause of Christ. And it is in turn a great privilege to him to 'serve to . . . just such slips of soldiery Christ's royal ration'. The First Communion is a principal milestone in a Catholic's life. The poem expresses the poet's joy at the occasion, and at his work whenever it encounters youth of this natural innocence.

The last four verses are darker, however. Earlier Hopkins has prayed that a guardian angel ('angel-warder') may 'squander' (that is, disperse and drive away) the 'hell-rook ranks [which] sally to molest him'. Now he reiterates the prayer for whatever will frighten off evil and lock love (religious devotion) in the boy. More painfully, and significantly, he asks that he may see the boy no more, for fear of disappointment. The boy's way seems straight before him, the poet cannot 'cry' (descry, perceive) 'disaster there'—

> but may he not rankle and roam
> In backwheels though bound home?

—that is, although he seems to be heading the right way (home; compare the homing pigeon image), may he not wander or backslide? I must leave that to God, the poet says (and God here is referred to as the Lord of the Eucharist, appropriately since a Communion is the subject of the poem), noting as I do so that I have prayed most fervently on the boy's behalf. 'Brandle' means 'shake' (compare French 'branler'); the strange last line—

> Forward-like, but however, and like favourable heaven heard these.

—means 'this was rather impertinent of me' (*forward-like* being another Northern colloquialism) 'but let it stand now, and probably (*like*) God heard my prayers favourably'.

In this poem Hopkins is very earnestly involved, and to most readers his meaning will communicate, in spite of considerable syntactical difficulty and some grotesqueness of rhyme and diction. ('Breathing bloom of a chastity in mansex fine', for example, is a most perilous phrase, though we ought to take it seriously and thoughtfully.) Hopkins's admirers have been distressed by his terse covering note on the poem when sending it to Bridges:

> I enclose a poem, the Bugler. I am half inclined to hope the Hero of it may be killed in Afghanistan.

(The boy had in fact sailed to the Punjab the previous month.) But far from debasing or exploding the poem this seems to me to confirm its painful seriousness.

Brothers is a slighter piece, a cheerful observation such as we all make from time to time (though not in verse) of instinctive decency or loyalty in children. The conclusion is that Nature (in this case *human* nature in particular), though 'framed in fault' (original sin) 'can be kind'. The conclusion is the least interesting part of the poem and reveals again how near such a poem approaches to a cloying sentimentality, crowing over children's behaviour. Such doubts do not disturb the reader during the earlier lines, because of their energetic Sprung Rhythm (three-stress couplets) and lively colloquialisms.

> Eh, how all rung!
> Young dog, he did give tongue!

The last poem to be dealt with in this chapter is *The Leaden Echo and the Golden Echo* (one poem, though the two parts were written perhaps at separate times). This is a Maidens' Song from Hopkins's unfinished verse-play *St. Winefred's Well*, and has certain differences from the other poems. It is of interest partly as a play upon sound, echoes and assonances being even more freely indulged than in Hopkins's usual verse; and partly as an extended account of Hopkins's attitude towards mortal beauty.

Is there any way, the Leaden Echo opens, to keep beauty from passing? Lead answers 'No'. The Golden Echo disagrees. There is one way, one key to the preservation of beauty: beauty must be given back to God, 'beauty's self and beauty's giver'. If this is done, every tiniest part of it will be kept

> with fonder a care
> Fonder a care kept than we could have kept it . . .

What does 'give beauty back' mean? From a reading of *The Windhover* and other early poems, or the 1885 sonnet *To what serves mortal beauty?* the probable answer is: we should enjoy mortal beauty but always recognize God behind it. God is what matters, and by being prepared to renounce beauty for the sake of God we ensure that we shall eventually meet unending beauty in heaven. In other words, if like Pater and the Aesthetics (see pp. 18–19) we see beauty as the end in itself, we shall restrict ourselves to the nightmare of *The Leaden Echo*, and become more and more depressed by the fact that mere beauty achieves no end, but passes and decays. If, on the other hand, we see beauty as a manifestation of God, and do not cling to it selfishly, we can be confident, as in *The Golden Echo,* of God's scrupulous care both of ourselves and of all mortal things:

> See; not a hair is, not an eyelash, not the least lash lost; every hair
> Is, hair of the head, numbered . . .

A minor but ominous detail of this poem is the harrowing line describing weariness and grating frustration:

> O then, weary then why should we tread? O why are we so
> haggard at the heart, so care-coiled, care-killed, so fagged, so
> fashed, so cogged, so cumbered . . .

That this was personally felt is clear from Hopkins's letters of the period. In a letter to Bridges in 1880 he wrote:

> One is so fagged, so harried and gallied up and down. And the drunkards go on drinking, the filthy, as the scripture says, are filthy still: human nature is so inveterate. Would that I had seen the last of it.

This prepares us all too forcibly for Hopkins's last years, in Ireland, and the sometimes desperate poems he wrote there.

6

Last Poems

In this chapter the last poems, written in Ireland, will be discussed in the probable order of composition. This differs slightly from the order in the *Poems* and other editions, and shows more clearly their grouping. Not that the poems of any one year are all of a kind; Hopkins was depressed during much of this period, but also resilient and courageous, and several poems show bursts of new cheer and experiment, amongst the prevailing gloom.

We may start our account of the year 1885 with two poems which in many ways seem to belong rather to the poems of the middle years. The first, the sonnet *To what serves mortal beauty?*, links with the Echo poems written three years earlier and discussed at the end of the last chapter. It is a complex and perhaps somewhat clumsy sonnet. The octet answers the question with which it opens by saying that beauty 'keeps warm Men's wits to the things that are', and illustrates this with the story of Pope Gregory whose awareness of Britain as a land to be converted really began with his glance at British slaves in Rome. The sestet advises men to reserve their love for their fellow-men; and says that beauty is to be observed, admired—and left to God (compare 'Give beauty back . . . to God' in *The Golden Echo*). The poem uses phrases which have by now become familiar, 'feature' and 'self', referring to the special Thisness of men's appearance; and assures us that man is God's highest creation and has the richest inscape latent within him:

> Our law says: Love what are love's worthiest, were all known;
> World's loveliest—men's selves. Self flashes off frame and face . . .

The Soldier is a generalized expression of the sense of nobility Hopkins felt (he says 'we all' feel it) at the sight of a redcoat or sailor. He says it is a manly, smart and sterling calling, and there-fore one tends to think the man himself may be so. Christ, the sestet says, has a special sympathy and understanding for the soldier, and even would be himself a soldier were he to come again. One may not feel much liking for the argument, but the expression is uplifting, comparing very favourably with Edwardian tommy-poetry.

The natural introduction to the dark, painful sonnets of 1885–89 is *Spelt from Sybil's leaves*, which was in fact probably the earliest, and is the least subjective. On the page this looks for-biddingly eccentric; Hopkins himself half-apologized for its appearance by calling it 'the longest sonnet ever written'. But, as he went on to say, the slowness and length of the lines is part of its method: 'it is most carefully timed in *tempo rubato*' (that is, a slack-and-swell freedom of rhythm which keeps fundamentally faithful to the metre). Apart from the length and the labouring rhythm, the sonnet is regular.

The first four-and-a-bit lines describe night, huge and oppres-sive. The magnitude of the infinite darkness is expressed by a first line composed entirely of adjectives, which convey both reverence and awe, but not peace-of-mind. 'Attuneable' means 'with things in harmony together, fitting'. The significance of 'earthless' will be realized later in the poem. After a rest, like a rest in music, represented by dots, the line runs into the next with the phrase 'stupendous Evening'. The night seems all-inclusive: birth, family-life and death are all within it. The setting sun is in the west, a 'hoarlight' (compare 'hoarfrost') of the moon is in 'the height Waste' (the vast other expanses of sky), and certain individual stars 'overbend us', giving features to heaven.

The next four lines tell how in the darkness earthly life has lost its various individualities (and so its inscape). The stars give features to heaven, but the features of things on earth are blotted out, blurred all together, they no longer even exist. Earth has 'unbound' her life—its very structure is dismantled. The 'dapple' of colour and individuality is lost, the colours run 'astray or aswarm, all throughther, in throngs'. 'Throughther' is a recognized dialect word, neatly conveying cramming together, being itself a blur of 'through one another'. 'Self in self' is soaked and beaten together. 'Disremembering' is Irish for forgetting, and it leads to 'dismembering', which again suggests the dismantling of the constituent parts of earthly existence. The poet addresses his own heart and acknowledges the justice of its fearful instinct, that is, the feeling that this is or represents *our* night or death. The word 'our' is stressed in Hopkins's manuscripts every time it occurs in this poem. 'Round' means 'reprove, or turn on'. 'Whelms' is the ancestor of 'overwhelms'.

This line and a half (from 'Heart, you round me right') is the simplest in the sonnet and the most gripping. The huge slow octet has established the oppressive image of immense blackness, and in these simpler words it is all made more immediate to us, and terrifying. Here Hopkins's feminine (two-syllable) rhymes seem to me to work superbly: the ease and rightness of 'end us' coming after elaborate earlier versions of the same sound show that these last words are the original and inevitable end to which the octet has been leading.

The sestet is a development, not a counter-statement. Boughs make patterns against the 'bleak light'; the leaves are like beaks and dragons, the light is cold and smooth like the steel of tools. The picture, which began soberly and without forceful emotion, is now unmistakably sinister. And it is 'our tale, O our oracle!'. A Sibyl was a prophetess, and the poem's title begins to be meaningful. The nightfall warns us of our future. Our future is death, and an after-life of either Heaven or Hell. (Gardner thinks there is a particular suggestion of 'the Cumaean Sibyl who conducted Aeneas into the underworld'). All life, at its end ('waned') has its variety, its 'dapple', 'self' and colour, dismantled: mortal life loses its complexity (the word comes to mind from W. B. Yeats's *Byzantium*, a poem of similar purport) and is sorted simply into good and evil. (The metaphors are, first, of unravelling wool on to spools, second, of separating flocks into folds—sheep and goats perhaps?) For sinful man this stark awareness, of death and the separation into good and evil, is terrible, and the poet feelingly exhorts us (or himself) to be 'ware of a world where but these two tell'. It is *thought* at its absolute and inescapable, without sheath or shelter to obscure its force for us: thoughts 'grind' against each other, and it is like a rack of torture for the mind.

This poem, which seems to me most impressive and moving, is not explicitly about Hopkins in person: it is about mankind, or even all earthly life. But the difference in subject and treatment from Hopkins's earlier poetry is striking. This is our first sight of desolation.

Hopkins's letter to Bridges of 17 May 1885 says:

> I have after long silence written two sonnets, which I am touching: if ever anything was written in blood one of these was.

There is no means of knowing which he meant. *Sybil's leaves*, *Carrion Comfort* and *No Worst, there is none* ... are of this time, and linked with these we may take *Poems* 66, 67, 68 and 69, for although no date for these is known, Hopkins wrote to Bridges on 1 September 1885:

> I shall shortly have some sonnets to send to you, five or more. Four of these came like inspirations unbidden and against my will.

The last phrase suggests poems of distress, which these certainly are. In short, it seems very likely that all the above sonnets are of 1885.

All are simpler in structure than *Spelt from Sybil's Leaves*, being regular sonnets of five-stress lines (six-stress in *Carrion Comfort*) where that sonnet has eight stresses to each line (in the first line the 'rest' takes one stress).

'CARRION COMFORT'

The title was provided by Bridges. This is, with *The Windhover*, the most dramatic of Hopkins's sonnets. The sestet tells us that an experience of suffering imposed by God some time earlier is being remembered; but the octet is in the present tense, and it is hard not to feel that the motivating force of the poem is a present crisis. To feast on Despair is like feasting on dead meat, carrion, the death of oneself, and is poor comfort. The poet refuses to give himself up to that: he is still a free agent, capable of hope, capable of resisting the urge to suicide. This first quatrain is simpler than the rest of the poem, and deeply pathetic, but tense nevertheless, both in the imagery and in the continually interrupting punctuation. The movement is full of effort, halting.

The second quatrain moves rapidly, in something like panic, as the poet turns from mustering his courage to the image of the terrible God who is angry with him. This is the giant of *Deutschland* 1-3, his right foot, which is powerful enough to 'wring' the world, rocking the poet's body; his limbs are like those of a lion; his eyes are grim ('darksome') and 'devouring', like those of a monster. Note the vivid 'me heaped there'—like so much rubbish, so much dust.

The first line of the sestet offers an explanation of the purpose of such suffering. It is imposed by God, to test and purify. And, the poem continues, since submitting to God (the rod of authority then becoming the hand touching and supporting—compare *Deutschland* 1 and 9), Hopkins has felt fortified and happy. The next two lines ask whose happiness is it that matters? Should the poet feel happy, or should he be content if God is gladdened? God and the poet are seen again wrestling together, and the last words of the poem reach a sombre horror at what purports to be the *memory* of that struggle. The darkness, we are told, is 'now done'. The bracketed 'my God!' before the final 'my God' is melodramatic (as is the whole sonnet) but also seriously witty, in the seventeenth-century manner: Hopkins shows how unthinkable it now seems that he should have fought against God, of all people.

'NO WORST, THERE IS NONE'
Here the 'last strands of man' which the poet refused, in *Carrion Comfort*, to 'untwist', have virtually slipped apart. It is a poem of pathological depression, which some critics attack as an indulgence in self-pity (in, indeed, 'carrion comfort, Despair'). That the poet pities himself is clear, and that he is engrossed in his

depression, which seems to him a 'world-sorrow'. But our knowledge of the circumstances of Hopkins's life, of his usual vigorous strength in writing and ascetic courage in living, surely makes a difference to our attitude. (What some critics distrust is the very *appeal* which poems such as this and the previous one tend to have. They are perhaps thinking of the artistic dubiousness of Tchaikovsky's frenzies, for instance, in the 'Pathetique' symphony. It is an interesting comparison, which I leave to you.) Yvor Winters has argued that:

> Hopkins has no generating concept, or at least offers none; since he cannot move us by telling us why he himself is moved, he must try to move us by belabouring his emotion. He says, in effect: 'Share my fearful emotion, for the human mind is subject to fearful emotions'. But why should we wish to share an emotion so ill-sponsored? . . . This kind of thing is a violation of our integrity; it is somewhat beneath the dignity of man.

My own comment here, not meant to be cynical, is that the concept of 'the dignity of man' may have to be altered. Moments such as Hopkins records in this poem are genuine human experience, known to many people at some time. Positive, admirable, life-enhancing the sonnet may not be; but it is as much an aspect of all of us as Shakespeare's *The expense of spirit . . .* or Milton's *On His Blindness*.

Winters's protest may be technically accurate (Hopkins does not, in this poem, tell us what's wrong); and it is true that a poem of this sort would have been intolerable to Shakespeare or Donne. But this is a case where biographical evidence, and the evidence of a poet's other work, must be admitted. We know that Hopkins is a man of very considerable courage and determination, and that he does not write poems idly or wildly. Knowing this, we cease to doubt the validity of the emotion in this sonnet, and we encounter it with due horror.

Only in the second quatrain, nevertheless, is there a hint of hysteria or uncontrol, and if the large claims of 'a main, a chief Woe, world-sorrow' seem a little wild, and the personification of Fury a little too like a pantomime demon, yet also in these lines there occurs the almost unbearably clear image 'on an age-old anvil wince and sing', which, it should be noted, implies even here that the tribulation is deliberately imposed (by God the blacksmith). We remember the earlier image, in *Deutschland* 10: 'With an anvil-ding And with fire in him forge thy will'.

In spite of the apparent blasphemy of lines 3 and 4, and the longing for death in the last line, we cannot say that Hopkins here has lost his faith. This is a cry of agony, but the poet is still submitting (and never ceases to submit). I have made no comment on the sestet, which is well-known and easily intelligible; it has already passed into the acknowledged great poetry of the language, and its firmness of rhythm and diction is itself a refutation of any charges of faint-heartedness which the octet may provoke.

'TO SEEM THE STRANGER LIES MY LOT'
This is a calmer, more balanced poem; and there is no question here, or in the remaining 'dark' sonnets, of the poet's dignity being found wanting. An end, now, to gasps and cries; in this poem and those that follow there is something like resigned acceptance. (*Thou art indeed just, Lord* . . . is obviously an exception.)

The poem sums up the isolation of Hopkins's life in Dublin. His own family are 'in Christ not near' (being Protestant), and he himself lives 'among strangers' (in Ireland). His friends and only potential audience are out of earshot (out of reach) in England. Above all, Christ seems hostile to him—'he my peace' has become 'my parting, sword and strife'. This is the real cause of the poet's desperation: he feels estranged from God.

The tone is humble and honest. He makes a self-rebuking qualification, like the firm sympathetic priest hearing another's complaint:

> Not but in all removes I can
> Kind love both give and get.

'Not but' is the colloquialism 'not but what'. But when he *tries* to give his love, in spoken or written word, something—either of heaven or hell—stops him. This is the first hint, in the poems, of his literary sterility, of which he complains in the letters. Having to 'hoard' his love, or having to see it 'unheeded' when heard (note the assonantal sequence here), leaves him 'a lonely began'. For the construction 'began' compare the word 'also-ran' in sport.

'I WAKE AND FEEL THE FELL OF DARK . . .'

The same problem is pressed home more terribly in this sonnet. The ferocity of the imagery, and the echoes, in the sestet, of barbaric ancient tragedy ('God's most deep decree . . . blood brimmed the curse . . . their scourge to be As I am mine, their sweating selves') make this one of Hopkins's most powerful poems. The octet speaks the poet's isolation, his inability to communicate with God; the sestet points the horror of this, that he is turned in hopelessly upon himself, a state similar to the state of damnation.

'Fell' in the first line means the hide of an animal (the secondary sense of 'evil' is present also). As such this is a sensationally horrifying line: darkness is a hot furred creature, touched when day and freedom were hoped for. The night, not yet over, has been full of such images. For this image of night (referring both to the 'fit of nervous prostration' and to the actual problem of sleeplessness) compare the whole of *Spelt from Sybil's leaves* and the words 'wish day come' in *Carrion Comfort*.

The second quatrain is more considered and removed from the first distress. The words are, Hopkins says, justified, not without support. But it is not only one night, it is 'years', it is 'life'. And God seems to have moved house; all the poet's attempts to contact him come back impersonally marked 'Not known'.

The sestet has an unmistakable impact. Note the appropriateness of the image of gall rising to the mouth—bitterness from *within*. The submission here to God is like that of the Greek tragic hero, submission because there is no alternative; the poet feels himself to be, like the scapegoat in tragedy, cursed in his very creation. The last three lines explain what the curse is. Dough needs an added agent to make it rise; without it all is 'dull', useless. The damned are like this; to exist in isolation, without God, is damnation. (This is a common theological view of hell). The 'scourge' or punishment is simply to be oneself, in one's own sweat, gall, heartburn, bones, flesh, blood. The last words 'but worse', in spite of a potential ambiguity, should be taken as a sober recognition that damnation *is* worse than his present state. Any other reading would make Hopkins theologically irresponsible, as well as a whiner; and there is no evidence for either.

'PATIENCE, HARD THING!'

This and the next sonnet are mildly consolatory. The horror is still glimpsed, but the poet's courage is uppermost. The octet of this sonnet is difficult, and open to varying interpretations. I think it means: Patience is a virtue not easily acquired: it must be won by suffering, 'war', 'wounds', 'weary . . . times' and 'tasks'. The man who asks for Patience ('Patience who asks'—a very Hopkinsian construction) is asking for tribulation. Patience comes eventually, like an ivy growing over ruins, when we have suffered defeats and discouragements.

Note in line 5 the image of Patience taking root; this recurs in two more late sonnets. Roots imply growth, sustenance, and the soil to sink in. Hopkins's world at this time is like a rocky desert, where one creeps under a boulder in a whirlwind (*No worst . . .*), with no better shelter and no land fertile.

The sestet opens with a controlled, very painful statement. The image of hearts 'grating' on themselves recalls 'sheathe and shelterless, thoughts against thoughts in groans grind' from *Spelt from Sybil's Leaves*. Yet however reluctant we are to suffer worse pain, we must still ask God to continue to bend 'the rebellious wills Of us' to him. At all times Hopkins submits to God's authority. The gentle last three lines express complete trust in the 'delicious kindness' of God, which is all the time being distilled in 'crisp combs' (that is, honeycombs). God above all is patient; for him, and therefore for the poet, it is the end which matters, and there is the consolation.

This is another example, if we needed it, of Hopkins's self-critical wisdom, which is usually so far from hysterical self-pity. In spite of the first line, self-pity is just what this sonnet rejects—self-pity and engrossment in oneself. 'Give yourself a chance', the poet says to himself; 'give yourself a rest'. If we regard depression (as we should) as an illness, this represents a turn for the better—which is not to undervalue the poem's humility and courage.

The octet is technically remarkable: by repeating words and ploughing sentence structure together (yet preserving clarity of thought) the poet creates, first, a treadmill—

> this tormented mind
> With this tormented mind tormenting yet.

—which exactly depicts the 'self-yeast of spirit', the circular introversions, described in the previous sonnets; and, second, a nightmare, in which the failure of the phrases to end satisfactorily (no noun after 'comfortless', no verb after 'day') depicts the unanswered 'groping' described.

> I cast for comfort I can no more get
> By groping round my comfortless, than blind
> Eyes in their dark can day or thirst can find
> Thirst's all-in-all in all a world of wet.

Just as the sea, unending water, mocks the sailor dying of thirst, so the punning repetition in the last line here mocks the agony of the subject.

The sestet opens half-smiling; the poet counsels his soul (whom he treats as a simple and humble 'Jack') in sympathetic colloquialism: 'let be'. The image of roots appears again. 'Size' means 'grow, find itself', and the colloquialism 'God knows when to God knows what' is, as always in Hopkins, meant literally: 'leave it to God'. God's smile (his favour and kindness) cannot be dragged ('wrung') from him by self-pitying cries. Rather it will come at times unexpected, in the same way as bright sky, suddenly appearing many-coloured between mountains, 'lights a lovely mile' and gives an interval of happiness. The problem here is the word 'betweenpie', which certainly needs a note and therefore offends some readers. To *pie* is a respectable, if archaic, English verb, as in *The Pied Piper* or Hopkins's own *Pied Beauty*; 'betweenpie' is simply a compound verb formed after the German manner. Odd, certainly, but it should not spoil the whole sonnet for us.

There are no sonnets known to have been written in 1886, nor in 1887 until September, which is the date of both *Tom's Garland* and *Harry Ploughman* (though Hopkins says they are 'touchings up' of earlier attempts). In these two poems he does not speak at all of his personal state of mind, and the intricate and bold technique suggests a new heartening of creative energy. They are not, however, among Hopkins's finest achievements, and comment here must be brief.

Tom's Garland is a sonnet 'with two codas' (see p. 124 for 'codas'). The subject is the unemployed. The syntax is, as the poet himself admitted, 'very highly wrought, too much so, I am afraid'. This comment occurs at the end of a huge paragraph explaining the poem in a letter to Bridges. Most editors print the paragraph in full in their notes. If you follow it closely it will indeed clarify the poem, but hardly justify the awkwardness. As always in Hopkins there are lively and impressive lines—the first three in particular—and the poem is of interest in being Hopkins's only expression in verse of some of his political concerns.

Harry Ploughman is another extended sonnet, but this time the extensions are what Hopkins called 'burden-lines'—extra half-lines interspersed with the regular lines of the sonnet, with an echo effect. The poem is a simple picture, uninterpreted: the inscape of a *man* described for once with the detail and richness Hopkins more often gives to the inscape of landscape. This sonnet, in spite of certain awkwardnesses similar to those of *Tom's Garland*, recalls *The Windhover*, not only in the shining of the clods of earth sliced up by the ploughshare (at the end of the poem), but also in the captured rhythm of strong action, in lines

12 and 13 ('He leans to it, Harry bends, look'). The diction shows again the resources of Hopkins's vocabulary, and the sensitivity of his selection. Note also the emphasis in the octet upon 'each limb' finding its 'rank' and 'deed he each must do'— the idea previously developed in *Poems* 57 and other poems, here used of limbs in the one body, confirming divine order there as in the inter-relation of men, animals, and landscape.

Equally complex and experimental is the 1888 sonnet, *That Nature is a Heraclitean Fire and of the comfort of the Resurrection*, but the greatness of the theme and its closeness to Hopkins's heart make it a more compelling work. This time there appear to be three codas, though Hopkins's manuscript says two, and the lines are leisurely, with six stresses to them.

Heraclitus, the Greek philosopher, taught that the physical world was all formed out of fire, and was in constant change. For Hopkins this is the departure for a poem upon mutability and mortality, prime subjects of poetry, with the Christian Resurrection as an unexpected reversal of the conventional lament. The first nine lines describe 'nature's bonfire': the physical world. More particularly, lines 1 and 2 describe clouds; lines 3 and 4 the play of light on houses and through trees; 5–9 the wind blowing dry the mud-ruts of carts and footprints (till eventually no mark of man remains). The world is a bonfire, endlessly burning.

But how terrible that man too should be dissolved and annihilated. Of all God's creations man is the noblest, and has the highest individuality, ('clearest-selvèd spark'). How quickly the inscape of him ('his firedint, his mark on mind') passes, as he dies. Death is huge, black, engulfing; and nothing of man remains.

For Hopkins the simple mention of the Resurrection is enough. He rejects misery. There is a brilliant glimpse of shipwreck and rescue (an image which inevitably, in Hopkins, brings the *Deutschland* to mind). The next lines ('Flesh fade . . .') are either imperative ('let flesh fade . . .') or concessional ('though flesh fade . . .'); the sense is the same. All things may indeed die, the world be consumed by fire; it does not matter. At the last trumpet, redeemed man is immortal ('What Christ is') because of

Christ's earthly life and death ('since he was what I am'), and the poor scrap of a soul becomes 'immortal diamond'.

These last lines have a majestic certainty rare even in Hopkins. The last line but one is, in its transition by association, a piece of virtuosity: 'Jack', Hopkins's generic name for Everyman, an ordinary fellow, leads humbly to 'joke'. This by assonance suggests Job, who does not appear, but his potsherd does (see Job ii, 8), and it in turn suggests 'patch', a scrap or fragment. 'Patch' by assonance introduces 'matchwood', which is flimsy and weak. The last leap, to immortal diamond, is of course deliberately *un*prepared: this as a sequel to the earlier phrases connoting feebleness and poverty forces into the mind the full significance of the Redemption. Out of *that*, Christ has made *this*. And the last line repeats the phrase in full confidence and finality.

Of the same year is the simple sonnet *In Honour of St. Alphonsus Rodriguez*, which was written to order but is also a poem in which the writer is deeply involved, since it praises the courage of a man who was constantly fighting 'the war within' himself. Rodriguez, a door-keeper, was believed to have been continually troubled by evil spirits. The first quatrain describes the honour won in ordinary warfare, the second contrasts the equal courage of a 'heroic breast' fighting spiritual battles in private, which gets no worldly glory. The sestet shows that, in Rodriguez's inward battles, God was conquering with glory.

There remains 1889, in June of which Hopkins died. There are three sonnets, all dated to the day. The first, dated 17 March, is *Thou art indeed just, Lord* . . . , which has as explanatory title the opening of Jeremiah xii (of which Hopkins's first three lines are a literal translation—which explains what seems otherwise an unprecedented protest by Hopkins against God). This is the only fourteen-line sonnet by Hopkins in which there is not a full stop and a considerable pause at the end of the octet. The poem develops more steadily and directly than most of the sonnets. There is not the backlash or answer which one has come to expect from a Hopkins sestet. The very point of the poem is the cry unanswered, the cry considered and reasonable yet still drawing no response.

The tone is hurt, but always respectful. 'Thou art indeed just ... Wert thou my enemy, O thou my friend ... O thou lord of life ...' The poet's trust in God is still firm, but he *does not understand,* and he must speak. The restraint of his protest, with desperation just beneath the surface, makes this for many readers the most moving of all his poems.

His complaint is that sinners thrive, while he is sterile. For the only time after 1883 there is a recurrence of the early imagery— spring, blossom, birds nesting—here for bitter contrast:

> birds build—but not I build; no, but strain,
> Time's eunuch, and not breed one work that wakes.

And for the third time in these last sonnets the image of roots recurs:

> Mine, O thou lord of life, send my roots rain.

In this sonnet alliteration and assonance are at a minimum (the first four lines lack these devices completely) and the result is coolness, clarity, and a tone of particular seriousness and restraint. The rhythm (and therefore the syntax) is Hopkinsian; the sound of the speaking voice, full of tension, hinting at the risk of outburst, gives form to the otherwise free continuity of the lines (there is no substantial end-stopping between lines 5 and 13). Whether this is an indication of a developing sobriety in Hopkins's verse, as some have suggested, or of the wish to protest with dignity and humility (contrast the frenzy of *Carrion Comfort* lines 5–8), or simply of the lack of energetic inspiration which the poet complained of, it produced a new, different achievement.

The sonnet, *The shepherd's brow, fronting forked lightning ...* (*Poems* 75) is dated 3 April; editors have omitted it from the main group of poems in the interests of consistency of tone, for this, exceptional in Hopkins, is a poem of the most bitter cynicism. The first quatrain recognizes the grandeur of heavenly manifestations—lightning and angels. These, traditionally impressive, are rightly revered. 'But man'—the second quatrain begins—'What bass is *our* viol for tragic tones?'. Gardner finds here references to Isaiah xiv. The general sense—that man is insufficiently noble for tragedy—is clear. The sestet opens with a Swift-like line expressing disgust at man's eating and excreting, and goes on to dismiss man and his wife as simply 'Man Jack'—nothing noble or distinguished—and 'a hussy'. The last three lines are about the poet. One line suggests grandeur: 'I that die these deaths, that feed this flame'—perhaps referring to his priestly or poetic function of observing and sharing in men's lives—but the poet then breaks off, and resumes in bitterness at himself also. His 'tempests' are 'tame', his 'fire and fever fussy', and life itself a 'masque'.

Hopkins's last poem, *To R. B.*, is an appropriate and final work, and it is fitting also that here Hopkins should have paid tribute to Bridges, whose friendship kept the poems for us. It is a very calm and ordered sonnet on the subject of inspiration. The octet describes the moment of conception (first quatrain) and (second quatrain) the time of gestation, which may be a period of years, during which the idea is shaped and developed, with the memory of the original inspiration still clear. The sestet laments Hopkins's own lack of this 'sweet fire', and offers an apology which, if understandably centred in the poet's distress, is worded with great dignity and poise (in the regularity of the iambic lines, evenness of the caesuras, and the balanced pairing alliterations).

> O then if in my lagging lines you miss
> The roll, the rise, the carol, the creation,
> My winter world, that scarcely breathes that bliss
> Now, yields you, with some sighs, our explanation.

All readers have felt the happy paradox which we find today in these lines. If ever there was a poet who captured 'the roll, the rise, the carol, the creation', it is Hopkins; and if his last poems are a statement of terrible desolation, yet they are created with a surer and surer mastery of poetic craft, which makes them, as certainly as great tragedy, an assertion of human nobility, and of the lastingness of art.

7

Other Writings

What remains of Hopkins's Oxford poetry is well worth a glance, as an illustration of the poet's Anglican piety and of his gradual growth towards the habits of alliteration and assonance. Among a number of religious poems, both sonnets and stanzaic, the most interesting are *Heaven-Haven*, *The Habit of Perfection*, and *Lines for a Picture of St. Dorothea*. Of this last there are two versions, which offer the clearest possible demonstration of Sprung Rhythm as against ordinary metre. The Sprung version is almost certainly later. The first four lines of each version may be compared:

> I bear a basket lined with grass;
> I am so light, I am so fair,
> That men must wonder as I pass
> And at the basket that I bear . . .

First version

> I bear a basket lined with grass.
> I am so light and fair
> Men are amazed to watch me pass
> With the basket I bear . . .

Second version

The rhythm of the second is less easy to grasp, but more vigorous; one feels more inclined, I think, to pay attention to what follows. What follows is, in fact, not of great interest.

Heaven-Haven is well-known, and of its kind masterly. Eight lines of almost entirely monosyllabic verse, with an apparently spontaneous and free rhythm which, when held together by the simple rhymes, is firm enough, incorporate a fabric of emotional imagery (storm against calm, hailstones against springs and lilies) which only a resolutely rational thinker might resist. In type and subject it is more similar, perhaps, to Christina Rossetti (whose poetry Hopkins liked) than to Hopkins's main work; but there is an entirely masculine strength about the diction and imagery, which the lady-poet does not offer. The second line omits the weak auxiliary verb 'do'—a practice normal in Hopkins's later verse—and the poem tends always towards alliterattion.

At the same time Hopkins wrote a companion-piece, *I must hunt down the prize* (*Poems* 88), which represents the man of action. It is even possible that the second poem (the tense is present or future, where that of *Heaven-Haven* is past) was intended as a progression from the first. At no time in his life was Hopkins inclined to escapism.

The Habit of Perfection is equally well-known. This is a most sensuous poem repudiating the sensuous life. Silence is the music the poet chooses; darkness for the eyes; bread and water for the palate; incense instead of perfume for the nostrils; stone for the feet, poverty for the body. The poet's leaning towards a monastic life is already hinted at, though he was still an Anglican undergraduate. The poem is a proof that the man who later wrote in bold rhythms and tortuous syntax was not incapable of producing a masterly poem in smoothly metrical lines (though the diction is already very idiosyncratic). The expression is superbly fashioned, standing out from Hopkins's other Oxford verse in its sure control of entirely original imagery and diction:

> Shape nothing, lips; be lovely-dumb:
> It is the shut, the curfew sent
> From there where all surrenders come
> Which only makes you eloquent.

Be shellèd, eyes, with double dark
And find the uncreated light:
This ruck and reel which you remark
Coils, keeps, and teases simple sight . . .

UNFINISHED POEMS

The fragments printed in *Poems* (3rd edition) would perhaps be
of interest however trivial their nature; in fact, they include
several poems of distinction, on which some comment should be
made. The verse-tragedy *St. Winefred's Well* was begun in
October 1879 and taken up again in 1881. Comparatively little
exists, but the intricacy of the poetry—resembling the middle
sonnets or, naturally, the *Echoes*—suggests extremely close and
careful working. One is more inclined to admire individual
phrases or lines than to be convinced by the emotions expressed;
Hopkins's thought as well as his manner is so personal that one
doubts if he was capable of giving a real dramatic life to fictional
characters. Like the other nineteenth-century poets who
attempted verse-plays (they nearly all did), he shows a vivid
sense of language and emotion, but little of character or active
situation. The fragmentary play does not make one greatly wish
it had been completed.

Ash-Boughs is undated but similar in style to the middle or
later poems. In early drafts it was a Curtal Sonnet, in the later
form it resembles the octet of *Harry Ploughman*, especially in the
rhythmic similarity:

They touch, they tabour on it, hover on it . . .
        With talons sweep
The smouldering enormous winter welkin . . .

It is more or less simply pictorial, though the preference
expressed at the end for May-blossom (as against December
boughs) implies a preference for life and growth, under the
guidance of God. Though unfinished, it is a lively and expressive
poem.

Another parallel between finished and unfinished poems may
be drawn between *The Candle Indoors* and No. 150, *The times are*

nightfall. . . . The latter is an unfinished sonnet in the chaster style of the late poems. Gardner sees it as 'a first sketch for No. 61' (*Spelt from Sybil's Leaves*), but I find this unconvincing; the clarity of the expression (which appears completely 'finished') in the first quatrain makes its own quite distinct statement:

> The times are nightfall, look, their light grows less;
> The times are winter, watch, a world undone:
> They waste, they wither worse; they as they run
> Or bring more or more blazon man's distress . . .

The sestet opens, however, like that of *The Candle Indoors*, with an introspective reversal: one can at least attempt to right the wrongs in one's own heart. 'Your will is law in that small commonweal . . .'

The poem lacks the last three lines, but ending where it does its aim is already acceptably achieved, and it deserves to be more widely known.

Epithalamion (1888) is a special case. The name means marriage-ode, and it was intended for the wedding of the poet's brother. What we have is a lively and free-running description of a young man bathing in a 'leafwhelmed' natural setting; the poem breaks off just at the point where the allegory of this is to be interpreted:

> What is . . . the delightful dene?
> Wedlock. What is water? Spousal love . . .

The bright gaiety of the early section is unique in Hopkins's Dublin poems: the shout of boys heard through woodland—

> . . . a shout
> That the hanging honeysuck, the dogeared hazels in the cover
> Makes dither, makes hover . . .

—and the fine description of their swimming and diving:

> With dare and with downdolphinry and bellbright bodies
>   huddling out,
> Are earthworld, airworld, waterworld thorough hurled, all by
>   turn and turn about . . .

This is known to the poet, a concrete experience which he can present as a brilliant image; but what it is intended to *represent* ('wedlock' and 'spousal love') remains to a great degree an abstraction for him, by reason of his way of life and temperament. The poem, then, is abortive, but it is valuable to us as an illustration of the descriptive zest which was still latent in Hopkins even in Dublin (the poem is drafted on university examination paper), but was normally repressed by self-denial or self-weariness.

Hopkins's best unfinished poem is a sequence of metrically-straightforward quatrains entitled *On the Portrait of Two Beautiful Young People*. This was written during a visit to Monastereven, a country house in Co. Kildare, where this (family) portrait hung. The opening of the poem is its weakest part. The fourth line is surprisingly akin to other and bad Victorian verse:

> And beauty's dearest veriest vein is tears.

The theme is similar to that of *The Bugler's First Communion*. Since the portrait was painted the children (a brother and sister) have grown up, and the poet cannot be certain that they have remained uncorrupted by 'the wild and wanton work of men'. Their expression in the painting, however, speaks of goodness and openness:

> She leans on him with such contentment fond
> As well the sister sits, would well the wife;
> His looks, the soul's own letters, see beyond,
> Gaze on, and fall directly forth on life.

Hopkins's knowledge of human character leads him away from any sentimentality; and in spite of such positive lines as the above, it is a sombre poem. Beyond ordinary moral choice or training he recognizes 'that leaning in the will' of a man, which seems immune to influence and lacking even a consciousness of itself: 'the selfless self of self, most strange, most still'.

The last stanza, though probably not meant to make an end, is a firm comment on what has gone before. As in other poems there is a mild self-rebuke: 'What need I strain my heart beyond my ken?' The poet cannot be God, seeing and bearing the burden of all lives. What he can do is 'bear my burning witness' against the corrupting influences of the world. The expression is controlled and earnest and not immediately like that of any other Hopkins poem. It is more satisfactory as a whole than the perhaps over-decorated *The Bugler's First Communion*; there is a more distanced wisdom about the later poem, probably because the young people here were not personally known to the poet.

JOURNALS

The *Journals and Papers of Gerard Manley Hopkins* (edited by Humphry House) is a superb book, which it is worth persuading your library to buy. It includes not only Hopkins's notebooks, Oxford essays, and Journals, but also the music of his song-settings, and fine plate reproductions of many of his sketches. These drawings, of which examples are reproduced in this book, are pleasing in themselves and offer a considerable guide to Hopkins's appreciation of landscape. What is most distinctive is the attention to detail, which is consistent with the theory of *feature* or 'sakes', revealing the special inscape of each tree, bird, or wave.

The diaries for the Oxford years, 1863–1867, are day-to-day notebooks in which sketches, fragments of verse, and botanical-artistic notes mingle with memoranda of books to be read and small sums to be paid. The interest of these is in their indication that poetry was always, for the young Hopkins, a day-to-day craft: these are apprentice notebooks of one who takes it for granted that he is training himself to be a poet. Most of these fragments of poetry are passages of nature-description, akin to the prose notes on flowers and skies, but there are also passages from verse-plays, and complete poems, which are printed in the *Poems* proper.

From Hopkins's visit to Switzerland, which started on 3 July 1868, his Journal develops an increasing richness of natural description, continuing thus till the last entry we have, in February 1875. This is the period of Hopkins's theological training, during which he had more time for study, observation, and meditation than at other times in his life, and during which also he was writing no poetry. The Journal becomes, during these years, his primary means of artistic expression. The notes on weather and landscape made there are not intended for public reading, but are nevertheless written with an abundance of craft in diction and metaphor. It is easy, with our hindsight, to feel that this is a deliberate continuation of apprenticeship, but at all times in his life Hopkins delighted in knowledge, and in coming to 'know' something on a sketch-pad or in words. He is noting information for himself; his ecstasy never alters or blurs his observation, which is always fresh. Wonder, for Hopkins, is precise as well as passionate, and this vastly increases the excellence of his Journal. Many passages have an interest far beyond the autobiographical. We not only learn that an experience excited the writer, but also discover the experience ourselves. The creative imagination at work is as keen as in many poems and more so than in much descriptive prose of novels. The whole Journal, 1868–1875, should be read if possible; I print here one extract from 1873 which may give some idea of its richness.

> April 8—The ashtree growing in the corner of the garden was felled. It was lopped first: I heard the sound and looking out and seeing it maimed there came at that moment a great pang and I wished to die and not to see the inscapes of the world destroyed any more
>
> April 17—To Whitewell with Mr. Clarke. Saw a shoal of salmon in the river and many hares on the open hills. Under a stone hedge was a dying ram: there ran slowly from his nostril a thick flesh-coloured ooze, scarlet in places, coiling and roping its way down, so thick that it looked like fat

Later—on Jeffrey hill at the cairn. Magnetic weather, sunlight soft and bright, colours of fells and fields far off seeming as if dipped in watery blue

The weather became cold. April 24 snowstorm. The birds clucked and scurried away under bushes

After a drought / at the end of the month rain

May 11—Bluebells in Hodder wood, all hanging their heads one way. I caught as well as I could while my companions talked the Greek rightness of their beauty, the lovely / what people call / 'gracious' bidding one to another or all one way, the level or stage or shire of colour they make hanging in the air a foot above the grass, and a notable glare the eye may abstract and sever from the blue colour / of light beating up from so many glassy heads, which like water is good to float their deeper instress in upon the mind

May 12—'Under the blossom that hangs on the bow': cherry blossom for instance hangs down in tufts and tassels *under* the bough that bears it

May 15—Arthur married to Rebecca Bockett. I heard from them at Folkestone, a two-handed letter

At this time weather very cold, on May 18 snow and on Pendle lying

End of May—There is a great crying of corncrakes at night

May 30—The swifts round and scurl under the clouds in the sky: light streamers were about; the swifts seemed rather to hang and be at rest and to fling these away row by row behind them like spokes of a lighthung wheel

June 5 etc.—The turkey and hens will let a little chick mount their backs and sit between the wings

June 15—Sunday after Corpus Christi. Some of us went to Billington to join in their procession. Mr. Lucas was with me. The day was very beautiful. A few streamer clouds and a grapy yellowing team moving along the horizon. At the ferry a man said 'Hāst a penny, Tom?'—the old ferry was below the rocks

June 16—Still brighter and warmer, southern-like . . . As I passed the stables later and stayed to look at the peacocks John Myerscough came out to shew me a brood of little peafowl (though it could not be found at that time) and the kindness touched my heart

8

Versification

Hopkins wrote at some length to explain his metrical and rhythmical practice. I am assuming that all interested readers will read his own Preface, which is printed with the poems. In this he is defending himself against charges we would no longer be inclined to bring—that his verse is slovenly or undisciplined. He therefore argues in the formal language of prosody (the study of versification).

It is unnecessary for the modern reader to follow this defence very closely: we are accustomed to much twentieth-century poetry which is less disciplined than that of Hopkins yet still succeeds; the influence of an American poet, Walt Whitman, for example, is widespread. Hopkins did not read Whitman's *Leaves of Grass* (1856), but was interested in Whitman because, from hearsay and from a few extracts quoted in reviews, he appeared to be a metrical innovator. If Hopkins had read more of Whitman's work he would have seen that it uses not a new metrical system but simply an absence of metrical system. The results of this complete liberty are frequently superb, but they bear no relation to Hopkins's theory or practice.

Today we shall not be worried by Hopkins's *freedom* of rhythm, but we must make sure we pay due attention to its *system*. It is important to remember how interested Hopkins was in music; I have already quoted the dictum of his tutor, Walter Pater, that 'All art constantly aspires towards the condition of music'. Hopkins's neat copy of *Harry Ploughman* is reproduced in this book, and shows the markings, analogous to those of written music, which the poet regarded as essential guides for the reader. We shall note also terms borrowed from music, such as 'counterpoint'. It is not too much to say that Hopkins was trying to write music in words. He obviously *declaimed* his verse, as many poets did at the time, thinking it quite another thing from prose. This is a method which most of us today dislike, and occasionally it may lead us to irritation with Hopkins's dynamic markings (for example, in *Harry Ploughman*, the stresses on the 'er' of 'shoulder' in line 5 and the 'in' of 'broad in bluff hide' in line 17). We are free, I think, to read Hopkins's poems how we like, but not to say that he was 'wrong' in places where his scansion seems unorthodox.

Some examination of his system is necessary here, and for this purpose a few common terms had better be noted and explained for those unfamiliar with the scansion of verse. Classical scholars and literary students will do right to skip this paragraph.

SCANSION means discovering the rhythm of a verse line by noting its STRESSED and UNSTRESSED syllables. The stressed are marked, in this and most books, by /; and the unstressed by x. A very light stress is marked by \. Traditionally, a verse line is considered to consist of several FEET, that is, small units containing two or more syllables in a certain pattern. Thus an IAMBIC foot, or IAMB, is as follows: x / (for example, 'the man'); a TROCHAIC foot, or TROCHEE, is the reverse: / x (for example, 'Hopkins'). Normally in the past a poem would settle into a series of feet of the same kind, with occasional but limited variation. Most English poetry is written in iambic lines, and also to a set number of syllables. In the IAMBIC PENTAMETER, for example, a five-foot line which is the commonest in our poetry, there must be ten syllables, five light and five stressed, and each foot must be either an iamb or a trochee; that is, no more than two consecutive light syllables or two consecutive stressed syllables are allowed. Rules being made to be broken, Shakespeare and others who use the iambic pentameter do depart from it, using feet of other kinds from those mentioned above, but they return quickly to the rules and never lose touch with the underlying form, which is called the METRE (measure).

SPRUNG RHYTHM

Hopkins's main innovation, in his theory of Sprung Rhythm,

was this: *no longer count syllables; count stresses*. Decide on a number of stresses per line and stick to it, but accompany them with as many or as few unstressed syllables, and in whatever position, you like. (The more light syllables accompany each stress, the quicker and lighter the line; the fewer, the heavier. See page 53 for examples of this from the *Deutschland*). Hopkins expounds this theory in terms of feet, allowing one stress per foot, but it is unnecessary to consider it that way, and the term 'foot' may now be promptly forgotten again.

The other devices introduced in his Preface are 'Counterpoint'; lines 'rove over'; 'hangers' or 'outrides'; and various rests or pauses. *Counterpoint* consists of 'putting the stress where, to judge by the rest of the measure, the slack should be and the slack where the stress'. This, as Hopkins says, is very common in the first foot of the line, for example in Shakespeare, Milton, and Pope; but is rarely sustained further, as in his own example—

> / x / x   x   /   x   /   x   /
> Generations have trod, have trod, have trod.

—where the metre appears to be the iambic pentameter, but the first four syllables form two trochees. The point is that the rhythm imposed by the poet upon the basic metre is heard at the same time as, and 'against', that metre, just as one hears two tunes at the same time in musical counterpoint.

A line is said by Hopkins to be *rove over* if its scansion is counted as continuing into the next line, from which it may borrow some slack syllables. The corollary to this is important:

> the scanning runs on without break from the beginning, say, of a stanza to the end and all the stanza is one long strain, though written in lines asunder.

This indicates Hopkins's approach to the writing of verse— he thought always of the listener, not the reader—and it explains his more startling enjambements, such as 'King- Dom' in *The Windhover*, as well as some of his rhymes, such as 'leeward' (pronounced, of course, 'lyoo-ud') and 'drew her Dead' in *Deutschland* 14.

Outrides are 'extra' light syllables, not to be officially counted. Hopkins ties himself in knots justifying this liberty to his imagined Victorian audience, but for a modern reader the concept is hardly necessary. Hopkins says also that 'the strong syllable in an outriding foot has always a great stress and after the outrider follows a short pause'.

Hopkins rightly says that Sprung Rhythm was common enough in medieval times (especially in *Piers Plowman*) but disappeared about Shakespeare's time, though he excepts the choruses of Milton's *Samson Agonistes*. The letters to Bridges of 3 April 1877 and 21 August 1877, and to Dixon of 5 October 1878 and 27 February 1879 may also be read by those interested in Sprung Rhythm.

One's real understanding of Sprung Rhythm comes in reading the poetry. *To R. B.*, his last poem, for example, is written mainly in regular iambic pentameters. The last four are impeccable examples of that form (though the punctuation of the last line, with the pauses implied, is highly personal). But although the first two lines of the poem—

> The fine delight that fathers thought; the strong
> Spur, live and lancing like the blowpipe flame . . .

—are each of ten syllables, the second would have been unacceptable to prosodists before Hopkins. The stresses fall on 'Strong', 'Spur', 'live', and lanc-'; three, in fact, fall upon three consecutive syllables (and soon afterwards come three consecutive light syllables—'-ing like the').

Again, line 10 reads:

> x / x / / x x x / x / x
> I want the one rapture of an inspiration.

The ordinary iambic pentameter (admittedly a very poor one) would have been:

> x / x / x \ x / x / x
> I want the rapture of an inspiration

Hopkins introduces an extra syllable (though by classical principles 'the one' could be elided and considered as one syllable), which demands a stress, which it steals from 'of'. The statement is more colloquial and more emphatic (the implications of 'one' being: that is *all* I need, just *once*), and the line no longer seems underfed.

A more complex example is the opening of *The Starlight Night:*

```
 /   x  x   /    /     x  / x  x   /
Look at the stars! look, look up at the skies!
 x  / x / x / x  / x x  x  /
O look at all the fire-folk sitting in the air!
 x  /   / x   x  / x / x  x  /
The bright boroughs, the circle-citadels there! . . .
```

Here, as very frequently, I think one has a choice. In 'look up' in line one either word might be stressed at the expense of the other, and in line two it is possible to treat 'all' as a slack syllable and stress 'folk' as well as 'fire'. This is not unusual in Hopkins, and although he himself wanted to print stress-marks and other notations (as psalms are pointed in the English prayer-book) to instruct readers, and critics wish to establish definitive readings, it seems to me to be the kind of choice we are glad to have.

I would go further and say that, especially in some later poems, Hopkins's stress-pattern does not in fact always operate. The sonnet, *That Nature is a Heraclitean Fire.* . . , is written, we are solemnly informed, in six-stress lines. For me this is an impossible gabble; I count eighteen stresses in the first two lines alone. This is to agree, perhaps, with Yvor Winters, himself a teacher of prosody, who describes Hopkins's accentuation variously as 'perverse', 'wilful', a 'deformation of the language', 'indefensible', 'grotesque', 'ludicrous', 'irresponsible', 'ridiculous', 'unpronounceable', and 'preposterous'. Winters advises us to read the poems 'in the normal rhythm of the language', though this is a 'melancholy compromise'.

This is more or less my view too. It is worth knowing, in many cases, what Hopkins's reading was (and Gardner's edition has helpful notes in this connection), because it may illuminate an emphasis of *thought* which one would otherwise miss (for example, the stresses on every 'our' in *Spelt from Sybil's Leaves*, or that on 'will' in line 9 of *Spring and Fall*). And we should attempt to observe these markings where possible in our own reading. But it *is* our own reading, and our first concern must be to make the poetry work effectively, which it may not do if we are fettered by a highly emotional nineteenth-century declamatory style. Most editors seem to share this view, by omitting Hopkins's markings from the main text of the poems.

But having said this, the difficulties are not so numerous as all that. The *Deutschland* is the poem in which rhythm has the most importance, and as a teacher I have heard many people new to Hopkins read that poem aloud without (if a Hopkinsian pun may be permitted) putting a foot wrong. (It must, of course, be read with *energy*, otherwise all fails). Where trouble arises is, more often than not, where the rhythm is not very strong, and is therefore less likely to be ruined by an error. Hopkins's rhythms should be enjoyed and admired, not worried over, and nothing should be allowed to put you off reading the poems yourself, to friends or to a tape recorder. Not to do so is like possessing the score of a Romantic symphony, yet never hearing it played.

CAESURA, END-STOPPING, SILENCES, ETC.

Hopkins's use of pause and of continuity is distinctive. On the one hand, his verse contains much *enjambement* (the running of syntax over from one line into the next, without punctuation), and this of an unprecedented liberty, that is, phrases are broken between lines, when no earlier poet would have broken them at all; on the other, he speaks for the most part in comparatively brief utterances, heavily separated.

As has been said, Hopkins regarded a stanza as a continuous unit, and the same is true of each section of the sonnet (see below). Yet in all poems except those with very long lines, the verse keeps its shape; the structure of the *Deutschland* stanzas or the early sonnets remains clear beneath the superficial variety. This variety is effected not only by the enjambement but also by the positioning of the *caesura* and other pauses. Caesura (marked ‖ in this book) is the natural pause which is held to exist in any verse-line except the shortest, though it is frequently so light as to be unnoticed. In most verse it occurs about the middle of the line, though its position is certainly flexible; in Hopkins it may occur *anywhere,* with some surprising results:

My own heart let me more have pity on; ‖ let . . .
MY OWN HEART . . .

like the ooze of oil
Crushed. ‖ Why do men then now not reck his rod?
GOD'S GRANDEUR

Often there are secondary pauses, as in the last three lines of *The Windhover*:

No wonder of it: ‖ sheer plod makes plough down sillion
Shine, ‖ and blue-bleak embers, │ ah my dear,
Fall, │ gall themselves, ‖ and gash gold-vermilion.

Sometimes the caesura or pause is of unusual violence, coming upon a full-stop after a stressed monosyllable (see 'Crushed.' in the example above), or at a turning-point in the poem; then it may be called *hiatus,* meaning a break in continuity, a real gap. Another example is:

Surf, snow, river and earth
Gnashed: ‖ but thou art above, thou Orion of light; . . .
DEUTSCHLAND 21

As I am mine, their sweating selves; ‖ but worse.
I WAKE AND FEEL . . .

In *Spelt from Sybil's Leaves* there are eight stresses to a line, and a 'rest' (that is, as in music, a place where words would normally be, but there is silence instead) of one stress in the first:

$$/ \quad\quad / \quad\quad / \quad\quad / \quad\quad / \quad\quad / \quad\quad (/)$$
Earnest, earthless, equal, **attuneable**, vaulty, voluminous. . . .
$$/$$
stupendous

The existence of a pause in a line is not in itself either a merit or a weakness. The strength of Hopkins's verse (in addition to the rhythmic freedom described above) is its variety. Compare several stanzas of the *Deutschland*, and note not only how the Sprung Rhythm gives interest, but also how enjambement and its opposite, end-stopping, are hardly ever the same in pattern for two successive stanzas (except that the last line is heavily end-stopped in thirty-three out of the thirty-five). Again, consider the opening of stanza 19:

> Sister, a sister calling
> A master, her master and mine!—
> And the inboard seas run swirling and hawling;
> The rash smart sloggering brine
> Blinds her; . . .

Here the first two lines have an exciting but easy swing to them; epigram approaches jingle (but note the enjambement 'calling A master', which makes the lines more distinctive). Jingle is dispelled by the consecutive stresses of 'rash smart sloggering brine' and the carry-over into the emphasized verb 'Blinds her', with strong early caesura following. This is violent, not easy, and the lines continue with urgent repetition, supported by the punctuation:

> but she that weather sees one thing, one;
> Has one fetch in her: . . .

Similar excitement is generated by the punctuation and the enjambement in lines 9–10 of *The Windhover*:

> Brute beauty and valour and act, oh, air, pride, plume, here
> Buckle!

But the skill of Hopkins's verse is equally remarkable where it is unobtrusive: the sestets of the sonnets are particularly admirable, both in the comparative orthodoxy of the earlier ones, where statements are smoothly extended over several lines, and in the more uneasy, broken lines of the later, where a series of clipped agonies interrupt the lines without destroying the verse-feeling. Any sonnet of Hopkins is worth studying this way. Here is the sestet of *To seem the stranger lies my lot*, where the uncomfortably heavy pauses are disturbingly appropriate to the state of isolation and sterility described:

> I am in Ireland now; || now I am at a third
> Remove. || Not but in all removes I can
> Kind love both give and get. || Only what word
> Wisest my heart breeds || dark heaven's baffling ban
> Bars | or hell's spell thwarts. || This to hoard unheard,
> Heard unheeded, || leaves me a lonely began.

THE SONNET

Thirty-four of Hopkins's forty-eight mature finished poems are sonnets. He uses the Petrarchan or Italian form, with the following rhyme-scheme (the letters stand for rhyme-sounds): *abbaabba cdcdcd* (the last six lines can vary in pattern). This is a taxing form, and furthermore there are strict structural divisions which may be observed and which Hopkins usually chooses to observe. Firstly, the fourteen lines consist of an *octet* (the first eight) and a *sestet* (the last six), which are traditionally separated by a full-stop and often by a gap on the page. Hopkins runs on from octet to sestet in only three sonnets, and even there the thought always changes in the eighth or ninth line.

Secondly, the octet may be considered (and usually is by Hopkins) as two *quatrains*, to be firmly end-stopped; and the sestet, similarly, as two *tercets*. Thus the basic form of Hopkins's sonnets, in addition to the rhyme-scheme outlined above, is 4 & 4; 3 & 3. It is strictly observed in eleven sonnets, and the *principle* is observed everywhere.

This is all very difficult to manage, as the reader may find out for himself if he wishes to try, and one asks why a poet chooses such a form and returns to it so often. The general answer is that a craftsman values a discipline within which to work. There is a framework, and a technical demand. The hard effort needed to form this correctly helps him to clarify his purposes and develop his intention, and the restrictions of the form save him from the more extreme misjudgments of taste, manner, and proportion.

More particularly, the sonnet was suited to Hopkins's poetry because the regularity and frequency of the rhymes prevent the reader, startled by Hopkins's original verse-devices, from losing the sense of the poem's shape. *The Windhover* without the sonnet-framework would be a much less satisfactory work.

The main tradition of the sonnet is meditative or imploring; it is static, not dramatic. Some of Hopkins's sonnets are of this kind (for example, *In the Valley of the Elwy, Spring, To seem the stranger, To R.B.*), but others describe, or even enact, emotional crisis. The only well-known precedent for this is in the sonnets of John Donne (1572–1631), which Hopkins probably knew, and with which his own are often nowadays compared. However, Hopkins's dramatic sonnets are also profound in idea (as are Donne's), and they make full use of the *stages* of the sonnet outlined above. Thus in most of Hopkins's sonnets the octet consists of the *presentation* of an event, a thing, or a situation, and the sestet offers an *interpretation* or *antithesis* or *new development*. This is entirely orthodox. Further, the thought usually moves on, to a new aspect, at the fifth line and twelfth line, as well as at the ninth. An appreciation of Hopkins's use of this form will frequently help in understanding the poem, and it suggests that, as James Reeves has said of his poetry as a whole, 'what has been hailed as an originality may be, rather, a profound traditionality'.

It would be unlike Hopkins, however, to leave the sonnet exactly as he found it, and in fact five of the thirty-four do not have the customary fourteen lines, while *Spelt from Sybil's Leaves* is so long that some readers do not recognize the orthodox sonnet-form which underlies it (and so they miss the structural strength of the poem). These variations are worth explaining.

Pied Beauty and *Peace* each have eleven lines, divided into six and (as Hopkins put it) four-and-a-half. This (explained by the poet in his Preface) is a new invention, which he called a Curtal Sonnet because it was shortened or curtailed, designed to offer the same discipline and proportion as the regular sonnet, but on a reduced scale, for simpler poems. The results are, I think, impressive; and it is surprising that the form has not been taken up.

Harry Ploughman is a regular Petrarchan sonnet interrupted by what the poet called, by analogy with song-refrains, 'burden-lines'. These are short echo-like extensions of the end of the third, sixth, eighth, and eleventh traditional lines. The device is interesting, but one wonders whether this musical decoration is really appropriate to Harry Ploughman, rather than to, say, the maidens of *St. Winefred's Well*. Along with 'lilylocks' and 'Amansstrength' it lends a suggestion of affectation to the poem, which is unfortunate.

Tom's Garland and the *Heraclitean* sonnet are regular Petrarchan sonnets with the addition of six lines (two being short) in the former and ten lines (four being short) in the latter, at the end. The added lines have their own rhyme-scheme, with the exception of the first, which is short and rhymes with the last line of the sonnet proper. These additions Hopkins called 'codas'. The word is familiar from classical music, meaning a tail-piece; but there is only one tail to an animal and only one coda to a musical movement, nor does a musical coda contain the first resolution of earlier problems—the real meat, in fact, of the argument, as happens in the coda of the *Heraclitean* sonnet. The technical invention in these two poems seems more or less irrelevant to their subjects. It may be simply because the poet found the traditional fourteen lines gave him too little space.

Hopkins's letters include many notes on verse, and also an interesting note on the sonnet (Letter to Dixon, 29 October 1881). In the absence of further space here, they must simply be given a general recommendation. It will be evident from Hopkins's poetry that he was outstandingly qualified to write on the subject.

9

Words and Word-order

Hopkins's early diaries contain numerous notes on words, notes
not merely philological but also intended for future reference in
poetic composition. His knowledge seems to have been, by 1864,
already considerable, as a result of close study. The following
entry, for example, appears in that year:

> In Slavonic *bugti*=terreo. cf. *Bug-bear*, *boggle* (North-country
> name for ghost), *bogy*, *bug*. Liddell and Scott connect φεύγειν,
> φυγεῖν, with Sanskrit *bhúg*, *bhúgámi* (*flecto*); Gothic *biuga*,
> (*biege*); Slavonic *bega* (*fugio*), *bugti* (*terreo*); Latin *fugio*. They
> might have added our budge which is almost identical in sound
> with the Sanskrit *bhúg*, i.e. *bhuj*. And perhaps *goblin* is for *boglin*,
> but of this I have no certainty.

In Hopkins's letters to Bridges there are three well-known
statements upon language which are essential texts for the reader
of Hopkins's poetry.

> ... it seems to me that the poetical language of an age shd. be the
> current language heightened, to any degree heightened and un-
> like itself, but not (I mean normally: passing freaks and graces
> are another thing) an obsolete one. This is Shakespeare's and
> Milton's practice and the want of it will be fatal to Tennyson's
> Idylls and plays, to Swinburne, and perhaps to Morris.
>
> 14 August 1879

> It [Barnes's English Grammar] makes one weep to think what
> English might have been; for in spite of all that Shakespeare and

Milton have done with the compound I cannot doubt that no beauty in a language can make up for want of purity.

26 November 1882

You say it [Doughty's poetry] is free from the taint of Victorian English. H'm. Is it free from the taint of Elizabethan English? Does it not stink of that? for the sweetest flesh turns to corruption. ... He writes in it, I understand, because it is manly. At any rate affectation is not manly, and to write in an obsolete style is affectation.

7 September 1888

The first of these quotations is perhaps the most important. Hopkins's excellence of diction is due not so much to his philological studies, which might (as the second quotation seems to suggest) have made him an academic purist, but to his good ear for colloquial usage, his sense of the varied feeling behind words. There are many examples one might choose.

Why, tears! is it? tears ...

DEUTSCHLAND 18

How it does my heart good, visiting at that bleak hill ...

THE BUGLER'S FIRST COMMUNION

He leans to it, Harry bends, look . ..

HARRY PLOUGHMAN

And in those places where Hopkins himself seems to be guilty of his own particular kind of 'affectation', a closer look will frequently reveal spoken idiom at the bottom. On page 88 I have already explained the apparently perverse last line of *The Bugler's First Communion*:

Forward-like, but however, and like favourable heaven heard these.

This is in fact a composition of North-country colloquialisms. Of course no Lancashire workman would speak this particular complex of words, but Hopkins's audacity can at least be said to be consistent with his own principles: the line is drawn from genuine and living stock.

Again, Hopkins's use of those innocent approval-words, such as 'dear', 'sweet', and 'lovely', which are normally considered to have degenerated so far through over-use that they are unfit for poetry, can also seem like unmanly affectation, and can in fact be traced to the same poetic principle of 'the current language'.

But Hopkins's imitation of colloquial speech goes further than the borrowing of words and phrases. His general method of poetic statement is unusually direct. His sentence structures are mostly brief and simple—simple in that they do not pile up subordinate clauses or balance lengthy phrases one against another in the cumulative, ordered manner of most poets. Hopkins's greatest sonnets, for example, consist of short, direct statements (the octet of *The Windhover* is only partially an exception), and *this* kinship to the speaking voice goes deep.

It may, in fact, limit the balance of thought, or its subtlety. Hopkins does not offer us the carefully qualified and related sentence-structures, giving an impression of mature consideration, which we find in, say, Samuel Johnson's *Vanity of Human Wishes* or Thomas Gray's *Elegy in a Country Churchyard*, and even in the more meditative poems of Keats or Wordsworth. Most frequently, Hopkins ejaculates. Where he does reason out an argument, the result is either somewhat dry obscurity, as in *Tom's Garland, Ribblesdale*, or *The Loss of the Eurydice*, or else a series of associated colloquial ejaculations. This second method has variable success. In the sestet of *To What Serves Mortal Beauty?* most readers find it so jerky and fragmentary that the rhythm and therefore the poetry are lost, but in *The Windhover* the absence of reasoned links between stages of thought seems fitting to the sudden and emotional revelations. Sometimes the very separation of each stage in the argument makes it easier to follow, especially when the 4 & 4 & 3 & 3 sonnet-framework is used in the separation. The clarity of *Poems* 57, the 'kingfishers' sonnet, is considerably due to the brevity of the statements.

Hopkins, then, is a poet who speaks for the most part tersely and directly, and who tries to use the idioms of his day. He is 'difficult' because of his use of archaic or dialect words, and—chiefly—because of his unusual syntax.

When he laments the lack of purity in the language, he in fact surprises me, for much of the strength of Hopkins's poetry results from his sensitive use of the variety English offers. Our language, though formed in several complex stages, may be divided approximately into:

1. Anglo-Saxon: the simple basic vocabulary of our lives, the words closest to our hearts. This includes Scandinavian and Germanic forms.

2. Words from French, which entered the language during the Middle Ages as French was used by the governing classes in England. These words come originally from Latin, but often sound more like Anglo-Saxon than Latin, e.g. beef, charge.

3. Words imported directly from Latin, from the Renaissance onwards. These were scholars' words at first, and in most cases have never quite lost their aura of coolness, dignity and intellectual distance. They are the words of science and exactness, not of warm emotion.

In terms of what most of us can recognize, it is perhaps safer to speak simply of English (Anglo-Saxon) and Latinate language, and admit that with words in category 2 we cannot always tell. We can all recognize the three or four syllable Latin words such as 'magnify' or 'resurrection', and the rougher English words such as 'wears man's smudge and shares man's smell'. We can all *feel* the difference between English *walk* and Latin *perambulate*, between *drunk* and *intoxicated*, between *struggle* and *contest*, between *deep* and *profound*, or between *lock* and *secure*.

Hopkins's poetry is unusually full of 'English' words—characteristically monosyllabic (in stem-form), with simple vowel surrounded by a profusion of strong consonants, including doubled consonant after a short vowel. This preference at once tends to make Hopkins's poetry forceful. Consider the most painful part of the sonnet *Patience, Hard Thing!*:

We hear our hearts grate on themselves: it kills
To bruise them dearer.

Here every word is English; and note in particular the three savage verbs: *grate, kills, bruise*. In such words there is a concreteness, an earthiness, an immediacy of sensation, call it what you will, which for an Englishman cannot be fully communicated by Latinate language.

These English words tend to demand more violent activity of lips, tongue, and teeth in their delivery. It is a Northern characteristic to speak consonants more fiercely than do the Latin races. Hopkins's poetry is always a structure in *sound* as well as in meaning. He wrote to Bridges, 'my verse is less to be read than heard' ... 'you must not slovenly read it with the eyes but with the ears, as if the paper were declaiming it at you'. This structure is achieved by the chiming of vowels and the alliteration of consonants, in a fairly heavy music which the French might regard as crude, but which is red blood to an Englishman. It is a strong, if unobtrusive, element in Shakespeare's more powerful verse:

> Poor naked wretches, wheresoe'er you are,
> That bide the pelting of this pitiless storm,
> How shall your houseless heads and unfed sides,
> Your loop'd and window'd raggedness, defend you
> From seasons such as these?

KING LEAR

> The barge she sat in, like a burnish'd throne,
> Burn'd on the water: the poop was beaten gold;
> Purple the sails, and so perfumed that
> The winds were lovesick with 'em ...

ANTONY AND CLEOPATRA

A closer connection with Hopkins can be seen in the medieval poetry of alliteration, and in Welsh poetry. In the fourteenth century Chaucer and the writers of the London region wrote a language much influenced by French, and this developed into modern English. Elsewhere, however, this French influence had not yet penetrated, and the convention of verse was alliterative rather than rhyming, perhaps for the very reason that the heavy consonantal nature of the local English lent itself to this device (and to onomatopoeia). The great English alliterative poems, *Piers Plowman*, *Sir Gawayne and the Green Knight* and *Pearl*, find their only well-known modern descendants in Hopkins's poetry. A few lines from *Sir Gawayne and the Green Knight*, a poem from the region which is now Cheshire, may help readers to see the link.

> Now neghes the New Year, and the night passes,
> The day drives to the derk, as Drighten biddes;
> Bot wilde wetheres of the worlde wakned theroute,
> Cloudes kesten kenly the colde to the erthe,
> With nigh innoghe of the northe, the naked to tene;
> The snawe snitered ful snart, that snayped the wilde;
> The werbelande winde wapped fro the highe,
> And drof eche dale ful of driftes grete . . .

This poetry was written to rules (one consonant alliterated per line, for example), which Hopkins did not choose to observe. But the passage illustrates the expressive possibilities of this diction, the consonants being thus emphasized.

> The snawe snitered ful snart, that snayped the wilde . . .

This is a vigorous communication of the idea of snow, though we may not exactly understand the other important words of the line. So with Hopkins's wreck:

> And the sea flint-flake, black-backed in the regular blow,
> Sitting Eastnortheast, in cursed quarter, the wind;
> Wiry and white-fiery and whirlwind-swivellèd snow
> Spins to the widow-making unchilding unfathering deeps.
>
> And the inboard seas run swirling and hawling;
> The rash smart sloggering brine
> Blinds her . . .

DEUTSCHLAND 13, 19

Literal comprehension of 'sloggering' is far less important than the associations called up by the word, just as we do not need to know what, say, 'snitered' means in the earlier passage.

When Hopkins wrote those lines he was in Wales, and had been studying the Welsh language and Welsh poetry. The complex rhymes and assonances which occur as frequently as alliteration in Hopkins's work are, we are told, a feature of Welsh poetry, where they form a system, with rules, called *cynghanedd*. Such phrases as 'Warm-laid grave of a womb-life grey' or 'the down-hugged ground-hugged grey' are essentially a transference to English poetry of the Welsh device (but again, Hopkins did *not* transfer the *rules*—he uses it exactly as and when he pleases). One almost takes it for granted as one reads the subsequent poems, yet there, at its least obtrusive, it achieves perhaps the finest effects, by the binding together of a line or a phrase, or the continuity of thought:

For Christ *plays* in ten thousand *places* . . .

POEMS 57

Why? That *my* chaff *might fly; my* grain *lie*, sheer and clear.

CARRION COMFORT

Together with these sound-devices, Hopkins borrows from the older and more provincial English a number of semi- or entirely obsolete words, or words belonging to a different dialect. This is certainly an obstacle for the reader (and one which seems inconsistent with the dictum that 'the poetical language of an age shd. be the current language heightened . . . not . . . an obsolete one'); but it is easily remedied by the explanatory notes which all editions make. The justification for the use of such words is their consistency both with the assonantal patterns of their context and with the subject-matter or setting of the poem ('throng', a Dales word, in *Ribblesdale*, 'voel', a local name, in the *Deutschland*, 'disremembering', an Irishism, in *Spelt from Sybil's leaves*). These words are too many to be listed in a glossary here, as

I should like to do. A few common ones may be mentioned. 'Dapple' and 'pie' are still known today, though scarcely in use. Both mean 'to colour a thing in many or mingling colours', and they represent the intricate richness of the external world which so fascinated the poet. 'Reave', meaning 'strip away, remove' is frequent, and so is 'reck' for 'think on, consider'. 'Hurl', a special favourite of Hopkins, is a case of a familiar word being used not so much in metaphor as in emotional suggestion, to create a feeling of violent effort. (*Deutschland* 2, 13, 15; *The Windhover;* etc., etc.) There is a link with 'hurly-burly', as is clear from the *Deutschland,* where we find 'the burl of the fountains of air' and 'wind's burly'.

The last example raises another point. If one suspects an association in Hopkins's poetry, the chances are one is right and Hopkins did intend it. His notebooks show how far he liked to explore the connections and suggestions of an individual word. The best place to examine the process of sound- and idea-association (and word-play) in Hopkins, because it is the least restrained and selective, is *The Leaden Echo and the Golden Echo:*

The flower of beauty, fleece of beauty, too too apt to, ah! to fleet...

Resign them, sign them, seal them, send them . . .

Finally, one must not underestimate the good use Hopkins makes of Latinate language when he chooses. His enthusiasm for the rougher English words does not become disproportionate or in any way restrictive. He values the longer Latin words, apart from anything else, for their fluid rhythm:

He was to cure the *extremity* where he had cast her;

DEUTSCHLAND 28

And the *azurous* hung hills are his world-wielding shoulder
Majestic—

HURRAHING IN HARVEST

Repeatedly (as in the second example) the *nobility* inherent in many Latin or French words is deliberately used, especially in passages about God. *The Windhover* is a notable case: Hopkins evokes court, kingdom, and chivalry in the words 'minion', 'dauphin', 'achieve', 'mastery', 'beauty', 'valour', 'billion', 'dangerous', 'chevalier', 'sillion', 'vermilion'. Again, Latin as the colder and more intellectual strain of the language is an important element in the first line of *Spelt from Sybil's Leaves:*

. . . equal, attuneable, vaulty, voluminous, . . . stupendous

The difference between one kind of word and another is perhaps most clear and most sensitively used in the close of *That Nature is a Heraclitean Fire . . .* where much of the point of the poem rests in the juxtaposition of 'common', 'mean' English words with a Latin phrase signifying glory:

I am all at once what Christ is, since he was what I am, and
This Jack, joke, poor potsherd, patch, matchwood, *immortal diamond*,
 Is immortal diamond.

SYNTAX

Hopkins's syntax is the aspect of his poetry which causes most difficulty and is, to my mind, least defensible. Even so, it is defensible to a great degree. Hopkins's attitude appears to have been (he did not write on this subject) that 'rules' must always come second to rhythmic or assonantal effect, and, in particular, that unimportant words such as auxiliaries and relative pronouns could often be omitted to make a line firmer and denser. Most of his oddities, therefore, are re-orderings or omissions, the result often being that he coins new verbs, nouns, or adjectives.

Occasionally it quite naturally is his purpose to startle. Stanza 28 of the *Deutschland* is a simple example; for the dramatic rendering of a crisis, sentences are broken off into mere hinting gasps. This is merely a heightening of a well-worn figure of rhetoric. More surprising, to a reader new to Hopkins, is the last line of stanza 2:

And the midriff astrain with leaning of, laced with fire of stress.

One may argue that 'stress' is understood after the first 'of', or that the 'of' could be omitted; either way the general sense is clear, and Hopkins has given an impression of confusion or panic by the broken structure. Again, in stanza 16 the sailor who goes to help the women is killed, and hangs on the rope in their sight:

They could tell him for hours, dandled the to and fro . . .

(*Dandled* means 'bobbed up and down'). This can be grammatically explained by the argument that 'to and fro' has been coined as a noun here, but what matters is that the listener is aware of *article plus adverb*, is disconcerted and distressed by what seems a mutilation of a sentence, and that such a feeling is entirely appropriate to the context. This example has always seemed to me to be a grisly invention.

So there are some cases of deliberate violence in sentence structure. More common is the re-positioning of words because of the demands of rhythm, rhyme, or idea. The worst example of this is probably 'To own my heart' in *Peace,* where the poet means 'to my own heart' but has reorganized the phrase to avoid the two weak syllables 'to my' together. It is disastrous because all readers and listeners will interpret 'to own' as an infinitive, and no amount of cunning in the reading-aloud can prevent this impression. But in the following line from *The Bugler's First Communion* the admittedly startling alteration in word-order produces a nimble rhythm fitting to the thought:

Those sweet hopes quell whose least me quickenings lift . . .

and in the first line of *The Candle Indoors* the placing of 'clear' after the noun, in the French manner, gives the word an application both to the noun preceding and to the verb which follows:

Some candle clear burns somewhere I come by.

Hopkins's verse seems easier as soon as one is accustomed to the omission of minor words. Many of his finest statements are verb-less, the verb 'to be' being understood (as often in Latin).

> I steady as a water in a well . . .
>
> DEUTSCHLAND 4

> Lovely the woods, waters, meadows, combes, vales,
> All the air things wear that build this world of Wales . . .
>
> IN THE VALLEY OF THE ELWY

The relative pronoun, 'that', 'who', 'which', etc., is frequently omitted not only when accusative, as is common ('the man I saw today'), but also when nominative, as used to be possible in older English (e.g. the Prayer Book 'to do that is righteous in thy sight', where 'which' is understood). This is confusing at first, easy when one gets accustomed to it.

> What was the feast followed the night . . .
>
> DEUTSCHLAND 30

> O well wept, mother have lost son;
> Wept, wife; wept, sweetheart would be one.
>
> EURYDICE 27

The second example illustrates also Hopkins's use of new constructions by analogy with old, most often confined—perhaps fortunately—to compound verbs, nouns, or adjectives, which can be quickly understood. The case here is more difficult, yet clear as soon as it is shown (as Hopkins showed Bridges in a letter) that 'well wept' is composed by analogy with 'well hit' at cricket; that is, 'you were right to do this and it was fittingly done'.

One must note also Hopkins's use of a past imperative:

> And the prayer thou hearst me making
> *Have*, at the awful overtaking,
> *Heard;*
>
> EURYDICE 29

—that is, 'may you have heard my prayer'. This is the construction which baffles us at the opening of *Henry Purcell*:

Have fair fallen, O fair, fair have fallen . . .

This means 'may he have fallen (that is, died) fairly (that is, in Grace, so as to be redeemed)'. The fourth line here illustrates again the omission of the relative pronoun: 'the outward sentence low lays him'. 'Which' must be supplied between 'sentence' and 'low'.

These two examples ('well wept' and 'have heard') show the importance of direct address and exclamation in Hopkins's poetry. This fits the ancient view of a poet as a public declaimer. Hopkins feels no self-consciousness in giving vent to the 'O' of poetic tradition, nor—and this is more original—to the placing of it *within* a phrase.

Complete thy creature dear O where it fails . . .
IN THE VALLEY OF THE ELWY

.. and with ah! bright wings.
GOD'S GRANDEUR

There is one more aspect of this subject to be mentioned. A reflection on the theory of inscape, as the poems and notebooks illustrate it, leads one to understand better Hopkins's often strange comminglings of words. Inscape is the realization of the essential quality of a thing, the unification of its many separate characteristics, and there is evidence that Hopkins was often attempting to do the same with the separate words of a phrase— words which, after all, are describing a *single* manifestation. ('Brunette', by such criteria, is a more satisfactory expression than 'girl with brown hair'.) Where there would normally be a noun plus relative clause, Hopkins often has a complex adjective or participle plus the noun. Like all his 'innovations', this is an extension of an already-current device, the compound adjective beloved of Keats.

The first words of the *Deutschland* are an example:

> Thou mastering me
> God!

—where the more expected structure would be 'Thou God who masterest me'. The phrase is as it were folded in upon itself, to create a single speech-unit. There are many and varied examples: 'wind -lilylocks- laced' in *Harry Ploughman;* 'the rolling level underneath him steady air' in *The Windhover:* 'the O-seal-that-so feature' in *To What Serves Mortal Beauty?;* 'Miracle-in-Mary-of-flame' in the *Deutschland*. The most extreme is 'Amansstrength' in *Harry Ploughman*, an admittedly eccentric word-creation, with the perfectly serious aim of capturing not the two-stage thought process 'A man . . . his strength', which the ordinary phrase must involve, but the *quality* itself, *one* thing, like, say, electricity or cheese.

One cannot cover here all Hopkins's departures from custom-ary speech; to note them in one poem alone would take much space. What this chapter has tried to do is outline the principles behind the divergences, and the commonest forms they take. The difficulty of Hopkins is, I believe, to a great degree one of the surface. Once one has cleared up a few puzzlements in a poem one can return to that poem with comparative confidence, and share the poet's creation more easily than one may the abstract difficulties of, say, Blake, or Eliot, or indeed Wordsworth. Hopkins's poetry is an experience for the ears first, and as such it offers immediate rewards and few lasting problems.

10

Imagery

Imagery—the comparisons and references which a poet chooses to make instead of always identifying something in the most prosaic way—is of vital importance in all poetry; and it has become a commonplace of modern criticism that the analysis of a poet's imagery can give a good impression of the underlying themes of his work, and sometimes of his character. Hopkins's imagery covers a wider range of experience than his actual poetic statement, and is certainly worth studying.

One may start with the most conventional (but not necessarily the weakest) images, those which religious poetry seems bound to employ. LIGHT for goodness and DARK for evil are fundamental in *The Candle Indoors*, *The Lantern out of Doors*, *I wake and feel*, *Spelt from Sybil's Leaves*, and the unfinished *The times are nightfall*. . . . God is repeatedly associated with FLAME (*Deutschland* 3, 23, 34, 35; *God's Grandeur*, *The Windhover*, *The Blessed Virgin Compared to the Air we Breathe*). The flame is sometimes a mark of God's terrifying power; in *Deutschland* 9 he is 'lightning', in *Eurydice* 28 'lord of thunder', and in *Deutschland* 10 he is enjoined to 'with fire in him forge thy will'.

The image of God as a GIANT is oppressive in the *Deutschland* (stanzas 1, 2, 3, 28, 33), and recurs in *Carrion Comfort:*

>   why wouldst thou rude on me
> Thy wring-world right foot rock? lay a lionlimb against me? scan
> With darksome devouring eyes my bruisèd bones? and fan
> O in turns of tempest, me heaped there . . .
> . . . the hero whose heaven-handling flung me, foot trod
> Me . . .

There are several references to the traditional ROD of God's authority; and linked with crises in which Hopkins struggles with God is the traditional image of STORM, and the more personal image of SHIPWRECK. This underlies both the poems of shipwreck, and recurs in the 'turns of tempest' of *Carrion Comfort*, and the 'whirlwind' of *No worst, there is none*. But it is at its most compressed and most impressive in the 'resurrection' part of *That Nature is a Heraclitean Fire*:

> Across my foundering deck shone
> A beacon, an eternal beam . . .

Inevitably the *Deutschland* and the late sonnets have many images of PHYSICAL SUFFERING. The whole of the first two stanzas of the *Deutschland* are on this subject; also in the early section we have 'the stroke dealt', 'we lash. . . ', 'flesh-burst', 'heart thou hast wrung', and the hammering of a man's body upon an anvil. The last image recurs agonizingly, in *No worst, there is none*: 'on an age-old anvil wince and sing', together with the body hanging on sheer cliffs and sheltering from a whirlwind.

In *Carrion Comfort*:

> Not untwist—slack they may be—these last strands of man
> In me . . .
> . . . my bruisèd bones . . .
> . . . me heaped there . . .
> Why? That my chaff might fly
> . . . the hero whose heaven-handling flung me, foot trod
> Me . . .

In *Spelt from Sybil's Leaves* the poet is on a rack—

> Where, selfwrung, selfstrung, sheathe-and shelterless, thoughts
> against thoughts in groans grind.

and this is echoed in the savage lines of *Patience, Hard Thing!*:

We hear our hearts grate on themselves: it kills
To bruise them dearer.

The whole sestet of *I wake and feel* . . . ('I am gall, I am
heartburn') is of this kind. *My own heart let me more have
pity on* uses metaphors of a man groping round a prison, of
blind eyes seeking light and of parched lips seeking water at sea.
In *St. Alphonsus Rodriguez* one finds 'gashed flesh or galled
shield', which links words in the same way as the last line of *The
Windhover:* 'fall, gall themselves, and gash gold-vermilion', and
also recalls *The Bugler's First Communion:*

In scarlet or somewhere of some day seeing
    That brow and bead of being,
An our day's God's own Galahad.

There is a disconcerting similarity in the apparently harmless
unfinished poem *The Woodlark:*

    crush-silk poppies aflash,
The blood-gush blade-gash
Flame-rash rudred . . .

And one may also note the painful precision of this, in
Binsey Poplars:

That, like this sleek and seeing ball
But a prick will make no eye at all . . .

The insistence of this imagery (most often applied to himself)
leads some critics to attribute an element of masochism to
Hopkins (that is, they suggest that he derived a pleasurable and
unhealthy excitement from inflicting pain upon himself, either in
reality or in metaphor). A simpler explanation is that the frail
Hopkins was forced to accept much physical hardship (if only of
illness) during his life, and was thus more likely to feel the force
and relevance of such images. The last line of *Deutschland* 2:

And the midriff astrain with leaning of, laced with fire of stress.

—is probably not metaphorical at all, but literally true.

The same explanation can be applied to his repeated admiration for the muscular body which he himself lacked (*Deutschland* 16, *Eurydice* 19–21, *Felix Randal*, *Tom's Garland*, *Harry Ploughman*).

There are many images of SIMPLE WORKING LIFE, images springing from direct observation rather than from literary tradition. The plough and ploughman in *The Windhover* and *Harry Ploughman:* the well in *Deutschland* 4 and *Poems* No. 57, the 'kingfishers' sonnet; doves in a farmyard in *The Starlight Night:* windfalls after a storm, in *To what serves mortal beauty?;* the lantern passing; the candle in a house seen from outside; the 'landscape plotted and pieced' in *Pied Beauty;* blossom heralding the mature fruit, in *The Bugler's First Communion* ('fresh youth fretted in a bloomfall all portending That sweet's sweeter ending'). *Felix Randal* is a convincing blacksmith, and Tom, with his mate, piling his pick before he 'rips out rockfire homeforth' (the nailed boots scraping sparks from the ground) is perhaps the only true navvy in English poetry (*Tom's Garland*). Describing the Heraclitean theory of the universe, Hopkins uses the very appropriate and unacademic word 'bonfire'. The clouds, in the same poems are 'heaven-roysterers, in gay-gangs'.

In scores of brief images Hopkins uses the vigorous concrete things of everyday life where weaker and more conventional images would have seemed adequate to other poets. Consider the word 'fastened' in *Deutschland* 1:

Thou hast bound bones and veins in me, fastened me flesh;

or 'brink' in *God's Grandeur:*

morning, at the brown brink eastward, springs . . .

Deutschland 4 uses the conventional image of an hour-glass, for mortality, but this time it is there, in the kitchen or hall-way, and one sees the sand running:

                    at the wall
         Fast, but mined with a motion, a drift,
         And it crowds and it combs to a fall . . .

To R. B. uses the workman's blowlamp as a simile for the
flame of inspiration. 'Fern' in *Inversnaid* is in 'flitches', a word
normally used of bacon; and the froth spinning on the water is
'a wind-puff bonnet'—a familiar image to the Victorian, though
not to us. The common and not inherently tragic affliction of
heartburn develops not only pathos but even grandeur in
I wake and feel . . .—

    I am gall, I am heartburn. God's most deep decree
    Bitter would have me taste: my taste was me . . .

—and the same poem uses one metaphor from the workings of
the postal service and another from baking. The poet's cries in *No
worst, there is none* are like cattle huddled together and com-
plaining; in *Deutschland* 27 long hardship is expressed in 'the
jading and jar of the cart'. Hopkins feels no incongruity, in *The
Windhover*, in employing both the courtly images of 'minion',
'dauphin', and 'chevalier' and the homely 'rung upon the rein'
(from horse-breaking), the skate on a bend, the plough in the
furrow, or the falling apart of coals in the fire.

Note the mighty and unliterary words 'wharf' and 'granite' in
Deutschland 32, the 'wheels' of weeds in Spring, the 'hurdle',
'broth', 'rack', 'scooped', 'rope-over', and 'barrelled' of the first
three lines alone of *Harry Ploughman*. Carrier-pigeons appear in
Deutschland 3 and *The Handsome Heart;* 'tram-beams' in *The
Candle Indoors;* the Host as a 'ration' in *The Bugler's First Communion;* winnowing in *Carrion Comfort*—the list could doubtless
be continued. Hopkins draws upon wide observation, with that
fearlessness of offending against decorum which is a feature in
Chaucer and Shakespeare.

When he uses traditional images, it is with extraordinary
freshness. The hour-glass has already been quoted. Another is
God as SHEPHERD, in *Deutschland* 22 (branding the lamb's fleece)
and 31 (a sheep-bell ringing sheep back). The sheep are real

sheep, not just a Biblical symbol. Death, again, is often compared to a REAPER, but rarely with so clear a picture of the growing meadow and the sharp blade as in *Deutschland* 11:

> Flesh falls within sight of us, we, though our flower the same,
> Wave with the meadow, forget that there must
> The sour scythe cringe, and the blear share come.

Similarly Hopkins repeatedly refers to the ROYALTY of God or Christ, and heaps up images of chivalry and heroism to accompany the idea. The ending of the *Deutschland* and the whole of *The Windhover* are the two most glittering examples.

The remainder of Hopkins's images are mostly of WILD LIFE, particularly vegetation and birds. The delicate beauty of a wing or a flower fascinated Hopkins, and the earlier poems are full of joy at natural life, contrasted with the towns of the Industrial Revolution. The sea, although mainly representing God's terrible power in the *Deutschland*, is also used in stanza 32 for his goodness—

> stanching, quenching ocean of a motionable mind . . .

—and in *The Sea and the Skylark*, as it 'ramps against the shore', it is an image of natural purity which shames the town. Streams figure in *Deutschland* 4, *Binsey Poplars*, and *Inversnaid*. Clouds, the sky, sunrise and sunset are often described in the Journals and play an important part in the poetry; for example *Deutschland* 5, and 26, *God's Grandeur*, *Spring*, *Pied Beauty*, *Hurrahing in Harvest*, *The Blessed Virgin*. . . and *That Nature is a Heraclitean Fire*. . . .

Two of these groups deserve fuller comment: the birds, and the images of spring and innocence. Birds are especially a feature of Romantic poetry; their grace and power seem to make particular appeal, from Shelley's skylark to the swans of Yeats and the French symbolists. Most important, birds *fly*. They leave earth and visit heaven and so are a traditional symbol of the soul—Angels or equivalent beings in various religions all have wings. But Hopkins wrote about birds because he liked them, not because they were a literary tradition; and so, as with the reaper and the hour-glass, they are real to us and in fact more likely to excite us with that original suggestion of heaven than are the birds of lesser writers.

'Thrush's eggs look little low heavens' in *Spring* is not a piece of plotted symbolism, but a vivid and typically colloquial appreciation of their colour and fragility. Hopkins's windhover represents mortal beauty at its finest and the glory of God is revealed in its flight, but it is still a windhover, and without the real experience of the bird there would have been no poem. In short, Hopkins is not a symbolist poet. The windhover has muscles and feathers ('a wimpling wing', 'the hurl and gliding') and so has the undefined bird-heart in *Hurrahing in Harvest*:

> The heart *rears* wings bold and bolder
> And *hurls* for him, O half hurls earth for him off under his feet.

The skylark in *The Caged Skylark* is a metaphor for the soul, but it is also a very real skylark, beating 'in fear or rage' against its cage. The skylark in *The Sea and the Skylark* represents natural beauty, typically strong and free. The stormfowl in *Henry Purcell* represents equal strength and freedom within the surging creation of an artist.

But birds also suggest peace, gentleness and the mothering wing, and are expressly introduced in this way. 'Not under thy feathers' in *Deutschland* 12, is a brief anticipation of the Holy Ghost in *God's Grandeur*, which—

> over the bent
> World broods with warm breast and with ah! bright wings.

—and the image recurs in *In The Valley of the Elwy*, once more associated with a sense of goodness protecting mankind:

> That cordial air made those kind people a hood
> All over, as a bevy of eggs the mothering wing
> Will. . . .

The fullest development of the image is the Curtal Sonnet *Peace*, which amongst conventional metaphor offers the rich verb here:

> Patience exquisite,
> That *plumes* to Peace thereafter.

There are no birds in the late sonnets, except in *Thou art indeed just, Lord*, where they are used as bitter contrast: 'Birds build—but not I build'. The imagery of natural growth and life is entirely absent after 1884, and this sonnet says very clearly why. It points to spring, the birds building, the 'banks and brakes . . . leavèd how thick! lacèd they are again With fretty chervil'. This fertility is what the poet utterly lacks. SPRING is Hopkins's favourite season, repeatedly mentioned or suggested in his earlier poems. It should be considered together with his delight in all INNOCENCE and YOUTH.

The sonnet *Spring*, which is the clear statement of this preference, may be irritating to the non-Christian. The analogy, though age-old, is fairly obviously false: summer is *not* more sinful than spring, and spring and summer are only a preparation for autumn. Hopkins of course evades this logical problem, and asks God to 'have, get, before it cloy', the spring-like innocence of 'girl and boy'. The thought is typically Romantic, but also very personally felt by Hopkins. *Brothers*, a short poem describing the natural loyalty of one boy to his brother, puts this emotional conviction against the contradictory dogma of original sin:

> Ah, Nature, framed in fault,
> There's comfort then, there's salt; . . .
> I'll cry thou canst be kind.

The Bugler's First Communion is another full statement of the idea, and the young bugler is twice compared to blossom (and the second time the image *is* extended to include summer and autumn—'a bloomfall all portending That sweet's sweeter ending'). *The May Magnificat* is Hopkins's finest description of spring; and there is a moving and deliberately nostalgic image of May as the nearest we know to heaven in *Deutschland* 26 (note the adjective 'peeled' in the fourth line, carrying complex suggestion of buds, freshness, and, perhaps, peals of bells). In *The Starlight Night* the stars are compared extravagantly to blossom. The growth of the young 'morsels of spring' in mild nights is instanced in *In The Valley of the Elwy,* and in the *Eurydice* (stanza 4) young men are the tree's 'bloom'. The significance of the title and the youth of Margaret in *Spring and Fall* is clear, and it is the young maidens of St. Winefred's Well who sing the *Golden Echo.* There this imagery ceases, and its importance to the poet is never clearer than by its long absence through the late sonnets.

In the end, perhaps, it is imagery which is the real life-blood of poetry (though each aspect of Hopkins's work has seemed to me the most important as I have studied it). Hopkins is a great poet both for his brilliant selection of images from the fullness of his observation and for the descriptive skill with which he brings those images to life. In spite of his considerable literary training (which can be dangerous in this respect) he uses imagery with repeated originality, and the consistency of certain patterns of images shows how directly they came from his emotional experience. A final comment might be that the richness and density of comparison in Hopkins's poetry is also unusual, and that all readers will find that deliberate re-readings, with responses prepared for the innumerable glancing images which underlie the principal ones, will be well rewarded.

11

Critical Views of Hopkins

Bridges's work in collecting, preserving, and eventually publishing Hopkins's poetry has earned him, since 1918, more abuse than gratitude. Certainly, the argument runs, we owe him our thanks for not allowing Hopkins to be forgotten and his poetry lost, but why on earth did he have to wait twenty-nine years to publish? What a difference a knowledge of Hopkins might have made to the 'Georgian' poets of 1910–14! What might Wilfred Owen have written, after reading the work of a poet he would almost certainly have admired? Matters are made worse by Bridges's imperious condemnations, in the edition of 1918, of Hopkins's 'faults of style', 'Oddity and Obscurity', and 'ellipses and liberties of . . . grammar'; by his somewhat condescending and pedantic notes, and above all by the 'emendation' which substituted 'moulds' for 'combs' in line six of *To R.B.* It seems clear enough from that edition that Bridges had no suspicion that twenty or thirty years later it would be he himself who was considered the quaint minor poet, and Hopkins the genius.

The defence runs as follows. Firstly, Bridges never fully grasped the excellences of Hopkins's poetry. The introduction by Charles Williams to the Second Edition explains Bridges's declining to continue the editorship by his being 'too preoccupied with *The Testament of Beauty* and feeling also that his own duty to his friend had been satisfactorily accomplished'. The word 'duty' tells us much. It is patent both from Hopkins's letters and from Bridges's notes that Bridges was baffled by much of the poetry. Being baffled he never realized what great poetry it was. Where he recognized splendour, he may have felt himself to be biased towards the poetry by being a friend of the poet. Secondly,

Bridges, knowing himself to be baffled, could not imagine a Victorian or even Edwardian readership taking to Hopkins (see, however, Dixon's reactions, quoted below); and thirdly, even his severe remarks on the poetry, in the 1918 edition, may be an attempt to anticipate the reactions of reviewers and force their attention beyond the 'faults' to the 'rare masterly beauties'. He says, at one point, that he enumerates the faults 'to put readers at their ease', which seems to support this theory. Bridges's reluctance to publish seems partly vindicated by the fact that the 1918 edition sold very slowly indeed at first. Finally, by 1918 Bridges was top poet in England, a public figure widely respected, and a book of poems by his friend was then likely to be easier to publish, and also more sympathetically received, than at an earlier date.

My own feeling is that we have more to be grateful for than to regret.

DIXON AND BRIDGES

The first reactions to Hopkins's poetry which we still possess are in the letters of R. W. Dixon. The more striking statements are quoted below:

> I have your Poems and have read them I cannot say with what delight, astonishment, & admiration. They are among the most extraordinary I ever read & amazingly original. . . .
>
> 5 April 1879

> The more I study your work the more I admire it: & the more I regret the fate by which, as Bridges says, it still 'unfortunately remains in manuscript', & seems doomed to linger there.
>
> 29 May 1881

> . . . you have such gifts as have seldom been given by God to man.
>
> 4 November 1881

I cannot but take courage to hope that the day will come, when so health-breathing and purely powerful a faculty as you have been gifted with may find its proper issue in the world.

28 January 1882

It may be argued that Dixon was a man stronger in generous than in critical instinct (he comments very little on details of Hopkins's work). His praise is always vague in terms, which may suggest an inadequate understanding. But it remains clear that he was immensely impressed by the new poetry.

Bridges's notes do tend to excite our irritation. They start with an introduction, the first two pages of which are the formal description of manuscripts and editorial methods. Bridges then goes on:

> Apart from questions of taste—and if these poems were to be arraigned for errors of what may be called taste, they might be convicted of occasional affectation in metaphor, as where the hills are 'as a stallion stalwart, very violet-sweet', or of some perversion of human feeling, as, for instance, the nostrils' relish of incense 'along the sanctuary side', or 'the Holy Ghost with warm breast and with ah! bright wings', these and a few such examples are mostly efforts to force emotion into theological or sectarian channels, as in 'the comfortless unconfessed' and the unpoetic line 'His mystery must be unstressed [sic] stressed', or, again, the exaggerated Marianism of some pieces, or the naked encounter of sensualism and asceticism which hurts the 'Golden Echo',—
>
> Apart, I say, from such faults of taste, which few as they are numerically yet affect my liking and more repel my sympathy than do all the rude shocks of his purely artistic wantonness—apart from these there are definite faults of style . . .

And so on. The phrasing of this could hardly be more off-putting to the hopeful reader of Hopkins if it had been written by a pronounced anti-Hopkinsian. The faults of style are 'Oddity' and 'Obscurity'. On oddity Bridges wisely allows Hopkins to speak for himself, which he does splendidly:

> No doubt my poetry errs on the side of oddness. I hope in time to have a more balanced and Miltonic style. But as air, melody, is what strikes me most of all in music and design in painting, so

design, pattern, or what I am in the habit of calling inscape is what I above all aim at in poetry. Now it is the virtue of design, pattern, or inscape to be distinctive and it is the vice of distinctiveness to become queer. This vice I cannot have escaped.

Obscurity is explained, but not defended, in grammatical or linguistic terms by Bridges. The rhymes come in for special attack. Their 'childishness is incredible'; they are 'repellent', 'hideous', 'disagreeable or vulgar or even comic'. There follow two paragraphs of qualified praise, ending with one really enthusiastic sentence:

> Few will read the terrible posthumous sonnets without such high admiration and respect for his poetical power as must lead them to search out the rare masterly beauties that distinguish his work.

The book was given reviews of varying degrees of sympathy and a general inclination to praise Bridges for his friendship rather than Hopkins for his poetry.

SUBSEQUENT EDITIONS AND CRITICS

The Second Edition (1930) was introduced in a more objective and twentieth-century manner by Charles Williams. There is no question of Williams's not having appreciated Hopkins's greatness, and the essay contains many insights. Hopkins and Swinburne are contrasted, to the former's advantage, and on the subject of alliteration Williams senses the inscape of words which this poetry often attempts:

> It is as if the imagination, seeking for expression, had found both verb and substantive at one rush, had begun almost to say them at once, and had separated them only because the intellect had reduced the original unity into divided but related sounds. . . . 'Cast by conscience out' is not a phrase; it is a word. So is 'spendsavour salt'. Each is thought and spoken all at once . . .

Compare the remarks on pp. 136–7 of this book.

Hopkins, Williams says, should be related to Milton because of their common 'simultaneous consciousness of a controlled universe and yet of division, conflict, and crises within that universe'. He compares the suffering in *Thou art indeed just, Lord* to that of Milton's *Samson Agonistes*.

One sentence in Williams's essay seems to contain an unintended and amusing clue to the growing popularity of Hopkins's poetry in 1930. The younger readers of poetry were newly under the influence of T. S. Eliot, Ezra Pound, the re-discovered Metaphysical poets, and others whose poetry offered an intellectual challenge. Williams writes, in the middle of a paragraph on diction and alliteration:

> It is true that we cannot make haste when we are reading him, but that is what helps to make him difficult.

Here 'difficult' seems to be almost an unqualified term of praise; and far indeed from Bridges's censure of 'Obscurity'. This is characteristic of the critical tastes of the 1930s.

The third edition (1948), which is standard today, was edited by W. H. Gardner, who also edits the Penguin selection and published (in 1944 and 1949) an exhaustive two-volume study of Hopkins's poetry. To Gardner's notes (especially on metre and rhythm) and scholarship the student of Hopkins is bound to turn frequently; their very thoroughness, however, perhaps deprives them of a sense of adventure or insight. Several Jesuit writers have published biographical and/or critical studies of their poet, the best being by W. A. M. Peters and the easiest introduction being by J. Pick.

The reactions of two great and original poets, T. S. Eliot and W. B. Yeats, are a little disappointing. Yeats, in his introduction to his *Oxford Book of Modern Verse*, recalls meeting Hopkins as a youth in Dublin, but receiving no lasting impression, and confesses to a lack of enthusiasm for his poetry. Both Yeats and Eliot seem more preoccupied than we should be today with the superficial 'innovations' of the poet, which, Eliot says (in *After Strange Gods*):

certainly were good, but like the mind of their author, they operate within a narrow range, and are easily imitated though not adaptable for many purposes.

He continues with what is to my mind a more damaging criticism:

a whole poem will give us more of the same thing, an accumulation, rather than a real development of thought and feeling.

1918 was perhaps a little late for either of these poets to have been helped by Hopkins (even if they had read his poems in that year, which is unlikely). Both had already formed highly personal and developed styles of their own. The 1930s poets, on the other hand, exhibit to excess their enthusiasm for Hopkins, in borrowed tricks which are unconvincing when stripped of their originator's total inspiration. The use Dylan Thomas makes of Hopkins is the most impressive, since his own response to the English language was lively and creative, but the results are still wilder and far less meaningful than those of Hopkins. More recent poets have perhaps made better use of Hopkins's example, as it has become assimilated into the general poetical heritage of the language: Robert Lowell's *The Quaker Graveyard in Nantucket*, for example, is written in violent, concrete language recalling Hopkins's wrecks and other poems (one notes a sailor 'with the coiled, hurdling muscles of his thighs'—compare *Harry Ploughman* and *Deutschland* 16), yet does not sacrifice its own independence of statement and character.

The most impressive early criticism of Hopkins came in notes and essays by the young Cambridge critics who did so much for literary studies between the wars: I. A. Richards (who used *Spring and Fall* in his experiments described in *Practical Criticism*), William Empson, who analysed *The Windhover* in his *Seven Types of Ambiguity*, and F. R. Leavis. Leavis's essay on Hopkins in *New Bearings in English Poetry* (1932) was written first and foremost to introduce Hopkins to those who had never heard of him and who were far less accustomed to technical audacity and intellectual complexity than present readers.

Leavis wrote in 1950 that 'powerful as his genius was, I should now feel bound to stress the limitations'; and in certain other respects the essay does not offer the full-rounded critique of Hopkins which might be expected today, now that the poetry is so widely-known. But it contains many good insights in a short space, and should be read. There are also two later essays by Leavis on Hopkins in *The Common Pursuit* (1952).

All these Cambridge critics, and almost all the innumerable others who have written (in America and other countries, as well as Britain) on Hopkins have done so in the most enthusiastic terms. Considering how much there is in this poetry which might be controversial, it is surprising how little resistance there has been to the rapid installation of Hopkins as the best poet of the Victorian age in England (ousting ancient favourites such as Tennyson and Browning.

In the 1960s and 70s, almost inevitably, a certain reaction against such a popularity has been emerging, it is true. The dissenting voices generally follow the argument thoughtfully laid down by Donald Davie as long ago as 1952 in his book *Purity of Diction in English Verse:*

> 'He has no respect for the language, but gives it Sandow-exercises until it is a muscle-bound monstrosity.... To have no respect for language is to have none for life; both life and language have to be heightened and intensified, before Hopkins can approve them.'

Still more uncompromising is the attack of the American critic Yvor Winters, in his book *The Function of Criticism.*

Winters is a celebrated modern teacher of prosody, and much of his essay is an attack on Hopkins's metrical theories. He has studied these carefully and, as it might seem, fairly, and his conclusion is that Sprung Rhythm is:

> a very complex accentual meter, in which the accents are for the most part the irresponsible inventions of the author rather than native elements of the language ... We frequently find ourselves

> forced into deformations of the language which are nearly un-
> pronounceable and are often ridiculous. This metrical method,
> moreover, is devised in the interest of intensifying an emotion
> which is frequently unmotivated or inadequately motivated
> within the terms of the poem. . . . Poems so constructed should
> be regarded as ruins rather than masterpieces. . . .

There is in the above complaint a hint of a recognition that
Hopkins's accentuations are those of a highly emotional declamation. Winters's criticism is bitterly anti-Romantic, and his
reaction against Hopkins may be taken as another reminder of
how very Romantic a poet Hopkins was. Winters attacks the
Romantic search for originality which manifested itself in
Hopkins, and censures the introversion and self-preoccupation
which are again Romantic characteristics:

> If we have a poet who is concerned with the expression of his own
> inscape (self-expression) and with the inscapes of natural objects
> and with little else, we may expect him to produce poems which
> are badly organized, and loosely emotional, and which endeavour
> to express emotions obscure in their origins and to express these
> emotions in terms of natural details of landscape to which the
> emotions are irrelevant. . . . Hopkins is a poet of fragments for
> the most part, and it is only if one can enjoy a chaos of details
> afloat in vague emotion that one can approve the greater part of
> his work.

Winters's summing-up challenges our own maturity of
response:

> Hopkins is a poet who will find his most devout admirers among
> the young. . . . The young as a matter of necessity do not know
> the best English poetry in sufficiently rich detail to be critical and
> are more likely to be impressed by novelty than achievement;
> they are likely to be somewhat emotional and therefore un-
> critical of emotion in others; they are likely to be given to self-
> pity at odd moments, and hence sympathetic with chronic self-
> pity in others. I am not one of those who find failure more
> impressive than success.

I have given prominence to the views of Yvor Winters, not because I agree with them, but because this seems to be the place to encourage a critical response to Hopkins. This book, like so many others on this poet, has inevitably been devoted primarily to the explanation of the poems and the story behind them. I have said a good deal in praise, little that finds fault; and there is a tendency for us all, at this stage, at the end of a study of so challenging a writer, to be intoxicated with our own discoveries, with having interpreted what looked so baffling, with having sensed what once seemed so senseless. If you turn from this book to the critics listed in the bibliography, you will encounter the same tendency. Yet discrimination, in our literary enthusiasms, is *always* important; and if, after subjecting Hopkins's poetry to a more strictly critical reading, you still find much that is admirable, how much more you will admire it and respect it.

What effect, for example, do Hopkins's experiments in style and diction have upon you once you are familiar with them? Do they add extra subtlety to the statement, or do they remain excrescences, at first fascinating, later irritating? And what about this problem of the violent and immoderate emotion, which Winters censures so strongly? Does *The Windhover* awaken respect, or only bewilderment? What should we think of *Carrion Comfort*? Again, it is not Hopkins's fault that his experience and range were limited; but how relevant, in the end, are his poems to us all, to humanity (for this must be the ultimate test of art)? How much does the dependence on Roman Catholic dogma hinder the *Deutschland* from being the great generalized application of faith to life which it was meant to be? These are questions which must have your own answers, not mine, (and my own enthusiasm for Hopkins has been given plenty of space earlier); but I hope this book will have helped you towards them.

Bibliography

TEXTS

Poems of Gerard Manley Hopkins ed. by W. H. Gardner and N. H. Mackenzie, 4th ed. (Oxford Paperback, 1970).

The Correspondence of Gerard Manley Hopkins and Richard Watson Dixon ed. by C. C. Abbott (Oxford, 1935).

The Correspondence of Gerard Manley Hopkins to Robert Bridges ed. by C. C. Abbott (Oxford, 1935).

Further Letters of Gerard Manley Hopkins ed. by C. C. Abbott, 2nd ed. (Oxford, 1956).

The Journals and Papers of Gerard Manley Hopkins ed. by Humphry House and Graham Storey (Oxford, 1959).

The Sermons and Devotional Writings of Gerard Manley Hopkins ed. by Christopher Devlin (Oxford, 1959).

Gerard Manley Hopkins: a selection of his poems and prose ed. by W. H. Gardner (Penguin, 1953).

Selected Poems of Gerard Manley Hopkins ed. by James Reeves (Heinemann, 1953).

BOOKS ON HOPKINS

W. H. Gardner: *Gerard Manley Hopkins 1844–1889* 2 vols. (Oxford, 1958).

G. F. Lahey: *Gerard Manley Hopkins* (Oxford, 1930).

W. A. M. Peters: *Gerard Manley Hopkins: A critical essay.* (Oxford, 1948).

E. E. Phare: *The Poetry of Gerard Manley Hopkins* (Cambridge, 1933).

J. Pick: *Gerard Manley Hopkins, Priest and Poet* (Oxford, 1942).

N. Weyand (ed.): *Immortal Diamond: studies in Hopkins* (Secker & Warburg, 1949).

BRIEFER ESSAYS ON HOPKINS

F. R. Leavis: essay in *New Bearings in English Poetry* (Chatto & Windus, 1948; Penguin, 1963).

F. R. Leavis: essays in *The Common Pursuit* (Chatto & Windus, 1952).

F. N. Lees: essay in *From Dickens to Hardy* (Pelican Guide to English Literature, Vol. 6) ed. by Boris Ford (Penguin, 1958).

H. Read: essay in *English Critical Essays, Twentieth Century* ed. by P. M. Jones (Oxford, 1933; World's Classics no. 405).

Y. Winters: essay in *The Function of Criticism: Problems and exercises* (Alan Swallow, 1957).

Index

These indexes do not attempt to list every casual reference to poems or topics, but have been restricted to those providing fuller information.

GENERAL INDEX